Skunk Hill

Skunk Hill

A Native Ceremonial Community in Wisconsin

ROBERT A. BIRMINGHAM

Wisconsin Historical Society Press

Published by the Wisconsin Historical Society Press
Publishers since 1855

© 2015 by the State Historical Society of Wisconsin

Publication of this book was made possible in part by a grant from the
Amy Louise Hunter fellowship fund.

wisconsinhistory.org

Photographs identified with WHi or WHS are from the Society's collections;
address requests to reproduce these photos to the Visual Materials Archivist at
the Wisconsin Historical Society, 816 State Street, Madison, WI 53706.

Front cover: Photo by Edith Klement, Arpin, Wisconsin, courtesy of Lester
Public Library of Arpin, Powers Bluff file donated by Fred and Germaine Pigeon

Printed in the United States of America
Designed by Shawn Biner, Biner Design

27 26 25 24   2 3 4 5

Library of Congress Cataloging-in-Publication Data
Birmingham, Robert A.
  Skunk Hill : a Native ceremonial community in Wisconsin / Robert A. Bir-
mingham.—1st edition.
      pages cm
  Includes bibliographical references and index.
  ISBN 978-0-87020-705-1 (pbk. : alk. paper)—ISBN 978-0-87020-706-8
(ebook) 1. Indians of North America—Wisconsin—Wood County—History.
2. Indians of North America—Wisconsin—Rites and ceremonies. 3. Indians
of North America—Wisconsin—Ethnic identity. 4. Potawatomi Indians—
Ethnic identity. 5. Potawatomi Indians—Rites and ceremonies. 6. Potawatomi
Indians—History. 7. Wood County (Wis.)—History. 8. Wood County
(Wis.)—Social life and customs. I. Title.
  E78.W8.B574 2015
  977.5004'97—dc23
                            2015003148

Contents

Acknowledgments

MANY PEOPLE HELPED piece together the story of Skunk Hill. Of special note are Potawatomi elders with memories of Skunk Hill, including Tom Kichcumme, Lillian Kelty, Eve Hopkins, Vern Wahyeopon, Vera Denny, and Carol White Pigeon Snowball. Most of these marvelous people have since passed away, but I am fortunate to have known them and to have heard their stories. I also had a chance to work with and learn from many others, including Skunk Hill descendants Brian Snowball and attorney Joe Young of Vesper, Wisconsin, as well as Rey Kitchkumme, former councilman of the Prairie Band Potawatomi, and Nettie Kingsley, former historic preservation officer of the Ho-Chunk Nation of Wisconsin.

Many others shared their remembrances of the community, including Albert Rokus, Mr. and Mrs. Norm Severt, the Graham family of Arpin, and Lyle Hamel of West Virginia. The Grahams, who lived just north of Skunk Hill, showed me a basket given to them by a Skunk Hill woman in exchange for a chicken; Lyle shared written remembrances of Skunk Hill after his family started a farm in 1929 when the people living at Skunk Hill were their closest neighbors. Others who helped by sharing information on Skunk Hill are Tom Williams, formerly of the University of Wisconsin–Stevens Point, Gene Byers, Thomas Becher, Catherine Woodward, the Lester Public Library of Arpin (Wisconsin), the Westboro (Wisconsin) Public Libary, Larry Nesper of the University of Wisconsin–Madison Department of Anthropology and the American Indian Studies Program, and state archaeologist John Broihahn of the Wisconsin Historical Society.

I would especially like to recognize the Snowball family of Wisconsin Rapids, descendants of White Pigeon (said to have been the leader of the Skunk Hill community), who not only shared much oral history and other information but also extended their friendship to me. The late Carol White Pigeon Snowball (No-pe-no-kwa) was an expert on Skunk Hill and the Wisconsin Prairie Potawatomi. She collected a large number of photographs of Skunk Hill people and places, some of which appear in this book. Her son Brian Snowball (Kish-nuk-to), starting in 1999, helped lead opposition to initial plans by Wood County Parks to thin the forest and make other improvements at Powers Bluff County Park. These so-called improvements were to be made without consideration for the effect the work would have on the remnants and burial grounds of the old community and on certain plants in the park used to make traditional medicines. The ensuing public controversy led to my involvement as Wisconsin state archaeologist to use oral history, historical research, and archaeological techniques to locate parts of the park that needed protection. The resulting study laid the basis for the subsequent listing of Skunk Hill on the National Register of Historic Places and for this book.

Brian Snowball has since become a close friend and provided me much biographical information about Skunk Hill and its people. His late son, Bobby Snowball (Ga-mas), assisted professionals using sophisticated remote-sensing technology called electrical resistivity to map belowground remnants of the site without physical disturbance.

I would like to acknowledge the assistance of the Wood County Park and Forestry Department, and especially former director Ron Arendt, who provided material assistance and much cooperation during the archaeological investigations at Skunk Hill and for their sincere efforts to resolve conflicts regarding public land use at Powers Bluff County Park.

I also want to acknowledge the assistance of professional archaeologists and other specialists who conducted fieldwork during 2000 and 2001 to confirm the extent of the old community and identify features—including possible burial locations outside of two marked cemeteries—associated with its use and occupation. The fieldwork was coordinated by my office at the time and was funded in part by a $15,000 appropriation to the Wisconsin Historical Society by the Wisconsin state legislature to provide objective information in light of public disputes about the extent and nature of the community.

The Wisconsin Historical Museum archaeology program and the Mississippi Valley Archaeology Center at UW–La Crosse conducted an intensive and rather arduous subsurface investigation (deep shovel tests at close intervals) of the north slope of Powers Bluff around the modern winter recreational area opposite the documented Skunk Hill village. The study found no evidence of previous Native use. Hemisphere Field Services of Minneapolis used remote sensing to examine portions of the main Skunk Hill community that had been covered by asphalt or where surface evidence had otherwise been obliterated. Soil specialist and geomorphologist Michael Kolb sampled many of the suspected disturbances or anomalies identified by remote sensing and other potential features using a small-diameter soil corer; he concluded that many were natural. Matthew Thomas and personnel from Archaeological Research, Inc. investigated and mapped a sugar maple sap extraction and boiling site, or sugar bush, that was a part of the Skunk Hill community. The various reports stemming from the archaeological work reports are on file at the Office of the State Archaeologist. In addition, the Wisconsin Historical Society retained Lampert-Lee & Associates, Wisconsin Rapids, to provide legal descriptions and maps of the two Skunk Hill cemeteries so they could be formally cataloged as burial places and therefore receive protections under the Wisconsin Burial Site Preservation Program.

Several people read versions of the manuscript from different perspectives and made corrections, additions, and clarifications. These are John Broihahn and Jennifer Kolb (Wisconsin Historical Society), Larry Nesper (University of Wisconsin–Madison Department of Anthropology), Rey Kitchkumme (Prairie Band Potawatomi), and Skunk Hill descendants Brian Snowball (Ho-Chunk/Prairie Band Potawatomi) and Joe Young (Prairie Band Potawatomi). Even with their assistance, historical writing necessarily involves many details that invite errors, and I alone am responsible for any that remain in this book.

Preface

A Storm over Powers Bluff

ON A SUMMER EVENING IN 2001, a violent thunderstorm swept over Powers Bluff, a prominent hill that includes Wood County Park near the city of Wisconsin Rapids in central Wisconsin. A large number of people had gathered in the main park building to discuss the future of that part of the park that had been an early-twentieth-century Indian community known as Skunk Hill, or *Tah-qua-kik* as it is known in the Potawatomi language. The hill became the center of controversy beginning with a tree-thinning project proposed by Wood County to manage the park forest.

Some area residents objected to the cut because they thought it would disrupt the ecology of the park. The opposition quickly spread to Indian people whose ancestors founded the community, many of whom are buried there. Concerns centered on possible damage to the site, including disturbing burial places and disrupting an environment that produced plants still used to make traditional medicines. These concerns eventually extended to other county plans regarding maintenance and upgrading of a popular sledding and ski hill on the north side of Powers Bluff opposite the old village.

Among those gathered to discuss the future of Skunk Hill were members of the Indian community, representatives of the Prairie Band Potawatomi Nation whose ancestors founded the village, and me, in my capacity as Wisconsin state archaeologist. I brought with me knowledge of not only the site but also historic preservation laws and strategies. Stimulated by the controversy, my office initiated a study in 2000 that included collecting oral histories, conducting historical research, and completing archaeological surveys to locate remnants of the community that would lead to a nomination of Skunk Hill to the National Register of Historic Places. That designation, once approved, would recognize Skunk Hill's importance in Wisconsin and American history and would afford some protection to the site, as well as the burial places documented under Wisconsin burial site protection laws.

The storm hit suddenly, with thunder, lightning, heavy rain, and hurricane-force winds. Amid the deafening thunder, trees could be heard cracking and falling, causing many of us to flee to the stone basement of the building. The storm over Skunk Hill paralleled the social and political storm that was brewing around the site, and I am sure that for some it signaled the unhappiness of the spirits with park plans. But subsequent days provided a different sign to me. As inspection of the storm damage to the park proceeded, the roots of a great many toppled trees revealed a hitherto-unknown part of the site: a dense field of artifacts such as dishware fragments, lantern parts, stove parts, and the like. The debris may have come from the Skunk Hill community or from a logging camp that preceded the Indian community. Whatever the case, the area had clear potential for better documenting the history of Powers Bluff. This information allowed me to expand the boundaries of the National Register nomination I was writing and pointed to an area that would be valuable for future research. The storm had revealed previously buried history.

Likewise, this book was born out of a storm of controversy, and it too reveals a history previously buried, or at least one that is little known. The story of Skunk Hill and similar Indian communities will be unfamiliar to many, despite the fact that it is an important part of modern United States and Wisconsin history. The story tells of a time when the American government, with the assent of the general public, made it illegal for some people to practice Native religion and rituals on lands reserved for the exclusive use of Native people. The story is relevant today, when religious and cultural intolerance continues in the United States and throughout the world.

Religious and cultural suppression has at times affected many people and ethnic groups, but a long and strenuous suppression was directed at the original occupants of the continent. Having failed to develop a solution to the many conflicts between the Native peoples of North America and the expanding Euro-American population that was consistent with Christian morality, the federal government imposed a new and harsh Indian policy between the 1880s and 1930 whereby Indian populations would be forced to assimilate into the American mainstream by various methods. Programs designed to undermine communal ethics in favor of individualism called for carving reservations into parcels of land to be owned by individuals, forcing mandatory schooling for children in boarding schools away from their homes, and eliminating the speaking of Indian languages and the practicing of traditional religions on reservations. It is no small irony that this program was implemented by a nation formed by those escaping religious and cultural oppression in Europe, one that promised religious freedom for all.

The crafters of the policy achieved much success. Millions of acres of communally owned reservation land were eliminated, most ultimately falling into the hands of white settlers. Indigenous languages were lost as English became the first language of many tribes. Many cultural practices disappeared, along with much traditional knowledge and valuable oral history. But through it all, American Indian cultures persisted. While Native people would have to suffer through further changes in federal Indian policy during the twentieth century, off-reservation ceremonial communities like Skunk Hill played an important role in keeping the cultural fires burning in Wisconsin through the harsh period of forced assimilation.

My own involvement in Skunk Hill stemmed from the controversy, but it also reflected my longtime research interest in the many off-reservation Indian communities that once flourished in Wisconsin. Tribes that had been divested of most of their lands by nineteenth-century treaties and the subsequent removals of many to reservations in the designated Indian Country of the eastern Great Plains formed new communities of their own. I saw Skunk Hill as an opportunity to find out more about these people and about a period of history that I first learned about in the 1980s, while working on a research project regarding an old Prairie Potawatomi village called Indian Farms near Medford, Wisconsin. That research introduced me to the remarkable story of the Drum Dance, or Dream Dance, now called the Big Drum; John Young, a Drum Dance spiritual leader in Wisconsin; and the off-reservation ceremonial communities established by disaffected Prairie Band Potawatomi and other Indian people so they could continue cultural practices without interference of federal reservation authorities. These were things I had never heard about, despite what I considered to be a good education in American Indian history and anthropology. While I was employed at the Wisconsin Historical Society, my colleagues and I documented other such communities that we were able to afford some levels of protection. Through all of this research, I frequently saw the name Skunk Hill mentioned in historical documents as a major Drum Dance ceremonial center.

This book tells the story of Skunk Hill within the context of sweeping events that were national in scope. The story is assembled from ample oral history, a rich historical record, and diligent on-ground archaeological research directed at confirming the physical area of the old community to ensure it would receive the necessary protections, which have since been established by Wood County. Of course, this is not the whole story, for as with any community, many specific memories and stories have been passed down through the families with their roots at Skunk Hill and are best told by the Indian people themselves. Yet what is presented here will open the eyes of many and, I hope, provoke a deeper interest in the history and fate of this community.

1

Skunk Hill
(*Tah-qua-kik*)

RISING ABOVE THE COUNTRYSIDE of Wood County, Wisconsin, Powers Bluff is a large outcrop of hard quartzite rock that resisted the glaciers that flattened the surrounding landscape as well as the subsequent erosional forces driven against it by thousands of years of the harsh midwestern climate (Figures 1.1 and 1.2). It is an appropriate symbol for the Native people who once lived on its slopes, quietly resisting social forces that would have crushed and eroded their culture.

Figure 1.1

Powers Bluff in Wood County, Wisconsin, looking northeast
Robert Birmingham

1

A large band of Potawatomi people established the village of Tah-qua-kik, or Skunk Hill, in 1905 on the top and south side of the three-hundred-foot-high bluff, up against the oddly shaped rock outcrops that topped the hill and protected the community from the cold winter winds (Figures 1.3 and 1.4). The names of these outcrops, such as Spirit Chair, recall the presence of the former Indian village.

Skunk Hill was the most prom-inent of several ceremonial communities in Wisconsin based around a cultural and spiritual revival movement known as the Dream Dance, also called the Drum Dance and now called the Big Drum, that swept across the Midwest and eastern Great Plains in the late nineteenth cen-tury. For consistency, and following Thomas Vennum's excellent book *The Ojibwe Dance Drum*, it will generally be referred to as the Drum Dance hereafter, and the special drum used during ceremonials will be capitalized as the Drum.[1]

Figure 1.2

Skunk Hill is in central Wisconsin near the town of Arpin. | Robert Birmingham

Figure 1.3

The rock outcrops at the crest of Powers Bluff, circa 1920 | Alphonse Gerend Photograph Album, Wisconsin Historical Society Archives; WHi Image ID 115098

Figure 1.4

This undated photograph shows a part of the Skunk Hill community near the rock outcropping. | Photo by Edith Klement, Arpin, Wisconsin, courtesy of Lester Public Library of Arpin, Powers Bluff file donated by Fred and Germaine Pigeon

First introduced in the late 1870s by a Sioux visionary named Wananikwe, or Tail Feather Woman, after an attack (often said to have been by the US Army) on her village in western Minnesota, the Drum Dance ceremonials and code of ethics stressed Native traditions and values but carried a new message of peace between different Indian peoples, and indeed all peoples.

As it has been for societies across the world, warfare had been a part of Native American life for thousands of years, but European and American intrusions greatly accelerated conflict as Native people were pushed into the territories of others, competed for ever-decreasing resources and land, and vied for trade with the Euro-Americans. One long period of intertribal warfare lasted from the early 1700s well into the 1800s between the Ojibwe of the western Great Lakes and the neighboring Santee Sioux as the Ojibwe expanded westward into Sioux territory.[2]

According to the visions or dreams of Tail Feather Woman, a special large Drum was to be constructed and drummed by several people, and this was to be accompanied by dancing, singing, oratory, feasts, and other rituals over a span of days. The Drum and its way of life were to be passed from tribe to tribe, with elements of an existing drum incorporated into a new drum. Significantly, the first people to receive the Drum from the Sioux were their old enemies, the Ojibwe.

The nucleus of many Drum Dance settlements in Wisconsin, some lasting well into the twentieth century, was composed of Potawatomi people. Some Potawatomi refused to be removed to the western Indian Country in the 1830s after the 1833 Treaty of Chicago ceded their land. Many more fled back to Wisconsin from their Kansas reservation to escape cultural and religious repression. While formed around the Drum Dance, the communities became the center for a variety of other traditional and complementary ceremonials. The ceremonial communities in Wisconsin became cultural refuges for the continuance of Indian customs, language, and traditional values from the 1880s to the 1930s, a period when federal Indian policy sought to eliminate Native American cultures through forced acculturation programs. As such, the communities attracted residents from other Indian nations, as well as numerous visitors, for seasonal rituals and feasts—thus enacting the sharing among tribes that Tail Feather Woman envisioned. In the words of George Amour, who lived at the McCord ceremonial community near Tomahawk, Wisconsin, in the early twentieth century, these were places where Indians could "continue the practice and preservation of their religion, customs, and tradition."[3] Members of the Skunk Hill community had purchased the land on which they lived using proceeds from the rental of reservation lands in Kansas. The lands had been allotted to individuals under the disastrous Dawes Act, or the General Allotment Act, passed by Congress in 1887, which sought to hasten cultural assimilation by developing the concept of private land ownership and thus undermining communal ethics.[4] The act carved the communally owned reservations into individual holdings, called allotments, that were given to enrolled members of the reservation with the expectation that they would become independent farmers like their non-Indian neighbors. The sometimes substantial amount of land left over after allotment was sold off. Some Indian people leased out their holdings to farmers and ranchers for much-needed income, and eventually poverty forced many to sell their land to non-Indians. In the case of the Prairie Band Potawatomi Reservation, vice chairman and tribal historian Gary Mitchell observes that much of the allotted land was too poor to farm.[5] By the time the Dawes Act was canceled in

Figure 1.5

Undated photo of Skunk Hill residents | Photo by Edith Klement, Arpin, Wisconsin, courtesy of Lester Public Library of Arpin, Powers Bluff file donated by Fred and Germaine Pigeon

1934, millions of acres of land originally reserved by treaties for the exclusive use of Native people had been lost.[6]

At the height of its occupation in 1910, Skunk Hill and its vicinity had a population of more than eighty people (see Appendix I) but expanded considerably during ceremonies that drew Native people from all over the region and as far away as Kansas. Most of the people living on the hill were Potawatomi, but the community also included Ho-Chunk, Kickapoo, Ojibwe, and Menominee who had intermarried with the Potawatomi or were attracted to the community by the Drum Dance way of life (Figure 1.5).

The community covered approximately fifty acres, extending from the crest of the hill down the south slope. At one time more than a dozen structures—log cabins, shacks, traditional bark structures, and

Figure 1.6

Skunk Hill residents circa 1920. Elders identified the woman in the center as Mrs. Frank Young and the man at the right as community leader White Pigeon. | Alphonse Gerend Photograph Album, Wisconsin Historical Society Archives; WHi Image ID 64640

Figure 1.7

Men stand in front of a traditional elm-bark structure at the upper part of the Skunk Hill community. | Alphonse Gerend Photograph Album, Wisconsin Historical Society Archives; WHi Image ID 113806

more modern clapboard houses—met the needs of approximately six-teen families and other individuals (Figures 1.6 and 1.7). According to elders, one elm bark structure was the home of the sacred Drum, and another accommodated visitors who came for ceremonies. Some of the structures were arranged around the heart of the community: two adjacent dance rings enclosed by wood railings, 100 and 80 feet in diameter respectively, where the Drum Dance ceremonies were held

Figure 1.8

The two leveled, earthen-banked dance rings are still clearly visible. This is the easternmost ring, eighty feet in diameter (see arrows) and now surrounded by trees. | Robert Birmingham

Figure 1.9

The rock-walled cemetery, locally referred to as the Indian Bill Cemetery, at the base of the south slope of Powers Bluff
| Robert Birmingham

(Figure 1.8). Two small cemeteries served the community, one on top of the hill and one near the south base, and low rock walls were built around them when the land became a park (Figure 1.9). The graves are unmarked but originally were covered by traditional log and wood-plank grave houses.

Despite the protection from wind afforded by the rock outcrops, the environment of Skunk Hill was not well suited for a settlement, and it is remarkable that the community was able to last for more than two decades. The soil is rocky, and the surrounding area, occupied by farms, had little in the form of wild foods. Small springs were the only source of water. In the late nineteenth century one nickname for the hill was Bald Mountain, since loggers had clear-cut the area in 1905, leaving only a few old-growth trees. The people of Skunk Hill nevertheless survived through a combination of traditional and cash economies. Small gardens were planted and whatever small game could be found was hunted or trapped. Income for some came from the sale or lease of reservation lands that had been allotted to them, and many took seasonal work, helping out on area farms or picking berries for commercial enterprises. The residents bartered handicrafts and community products such as baskets, beadwork, and maple sugar for food and other necessities.

Area newspapers treated the hill as a curiosity and kept track of major ceremonies and other activities. Handheld cameras had been around since the 1870s, but in 1888 George Eastman invented and marketed the Kodak with the first rolled photograph film. In 1900 his Eastman-Kodak Company began selling the small and inexpensive Brownie, which greatly increased accessibility of cameras for the general public.[7] Some photographers found that Indian people, often dressed in elaborate ceremonial regalia, made interesting and exotic subjects for the photographs, which could be sold as postcards to tourists and others.[8] Skunk Hill and its people became popular subjects for these new photographers, resulting in a rich photographic record. Community members graciously posed for pictures, but the ceremonies themselves remained private affairs.

Historians and anthropologists, both professional and amateur, came to the hill or collected information about its people to document the unique and seemingly anachronistic community, sometimes referring to the Drum Dance as a religion because of the pervasive role it played in life there. Among these were Charles Brown of the State Historical Society of Wisconsin, anthropologists from the Milwaukee

Public Museum, and Alphonse Gerend, a dentist originally from She-boygan, Wisconsin, who took a particular interest in the Wisconsin Potawatomi. Gerend provided detailed descriptions of the community and took photographs, many of which illustrate this book.[9]

Through time the community dwindled as some founders died and other members moved elsewhere to find work and a better living. Some moved to another large ceremonial community called McCord in Oneida County, Wisconsin. Only sixteen people lived at Skunk Hill in 1928, and the land passed out of Indian hands in the early 1930s.[10] By this time the need for off-reservation ceremonial communities was also passing. The Meriam Report of 1928, produced by the Institute for Government Research (Brookings Institution) under the direction of Lewis Meriam and submitted to the secretary of the interior, harsh-ly criticized the treatment of Native people as a result of forced accul-turation programs and called for radical changes in US Indian policy. Contrary to the goals and expectations of the programs, the first sen-tence of the report bluntly stated that "the vast majority of Indians are poor, even extremely poor, and have not adjusted to the economic and social system of the dominant white civilization."[11] As a result, the federal Indian Reorganization Act of 1934 offered a "New Deal" for Indian people that canceled the policies of forced assimilation and provided the opportunity for federally recognized Indian nations to form their own constitutions and governments, albeit modeled on American-style governance.[12]

Native people would face other severe challenges from changing US Indian policies throughout the twentieth century, but places like Skunk Hill kept the cultural fires burning through a particularly harsh period of suppression. Many of the descendants of Skunk Hill, in fact, did not move far away, and today they form a vital Native com-munity on the outskirts of the city of Wisconsin Rapids, only six miles from Skunk Hill. Here the Drum Dance in its modern form, the Big Drum, continues to be a way of life.

In 1936, Wood County established Powers Bluff County Park around the upper part of the former Skunk Hill community, devel-oping a ski and sledding hill on the north slope opposite the old

Figure 1.10

Part of the winter recreational area on the north slope of Powers Bluff | Robert Birmingham

village (Figure 1.10). However, remnants of the community are scattered throughout the forest on the south slope within the park; the most visible to visitors are the two rock-walled cemeteries and the two earthen-banked dance rings. These humble vestiges belie the community's importance in Wisconsin, and, indeed, in national history. Organized around the Drum Dance, Skunk Hill was a vital ceremonial center that kept alive Native traditions and language during a time when they were rapidly disappearing elsewhere due to US government-sponsored forced assimilation policies.

2

Treaties, Removals, and the Great Suppression

SKUNK HILL AND OTHER ceremonial communities in Wisconsin have their ultimate origin in a long period of changing federal policy dealing with the "Indian Problem"—the fact that the lands upon which the American nation was being built were already occupied by hundreds of indigenous nations.[1] When the British were no longer in power, the new American government did indeed recognize the many different Native peoples as sovereign nations. Starting in the 1780s, they therefore entered into agreements with them through treaties for many purposes, but especially for the acquisition of land for white settlement. Lands were ceded in exchange for annual payments of goods and cash, called annuities, spread out over an agreed-upon length of time.

The treaties, however, were tainted by coercion, fraud, and misunderstanding. Land ownership was a foreign concept to the Native people, who saw the land as something that could be used, even exclusively, but not owned and sold. Further, tribal consensus was needed for important agreements, not just the approval of often carefully selected leaders, as was many times the case. The treaty era formally ended in 1879 when most of the Indian land in the United States had been acquired and most Native people placed on reservations where federal policy turned to eliminating Native nations by absorbing people into the American mainstream by force.

Reservations and Removals

Some American leaders, such as Thomas Jefferson, first envisioned that Native people could be encouraged to assimilate by various devices. But as violent conflicts in the east continued—for example, in the Ohio River valley, in the southeast, and as a result of the War of 1812 that found many tribes siding with the British—Jefferson himself began to promote the idea of segregation between the two groups that would give Native people a place to live undisturbed as they proceeded at their own pace on what he thought to be the inevitable path to civilization.[2] But the government's real interest was to make way for white settlement by removing Indian people. Congress passed the Indian Removal Act in 1830, and former "Indian fighter" President Andrew Jackson signed into law the plan to relocate all Native people living east of the Mississippi River, including those in what is now the state of Wisconsin, to a designated Indian territory in the eastern Great Plains, primarily the present states of Nebraska, Oklahoma, and Kansas. The reservation land, commonly known as Indian Country, would be held in trust for the tribes by the United States government.

Perhaps the most storied forced removal involved the Cherokee Nation of Alabama, Georgia, and North Carolina. A few Cherokee leaders signed a treaty agreeing to the removal without the consent of the tribe as a whole, and as a consequence thousands were force-marched to Oklahoma by the US Army. An estimated four thousand died along the way in an event the Cherokee called the Trail of Tears.[3] Many other Indian people of eastern North America endured their own mournful trails, including the Ho-Chunk of Wisconsin and many Potawatomi who were similarly forced to relocate to western reservations. In another instance of terrible suffering and death, a planned removal of Ojibwe living in Wisconsin and Michigan to Minnesota in 1850, ordered by President Millard Fillmore, was initiated by changing the location of the fall tribal annuity payments from Madeline Island in Lake Superior to the more isolated Sandy Lake in northern Minnesota. The annuities did not come until the following spring, forcing thousands to spend the harsh Minnesota winter without adequate food and supplies and resulting in many deaths. More died on the long and arduous trips back to their villages. In all, several hundred Ojibwe lost their lives to starvation, exposure, and illness. Subsequently, Ojibwe chiefs went to Washington, DC, in 1852 to argue to President Fillmore that the Ojibwe understanding of previous treaties was that they could stay in their homelands and even hunt, gather, and fish on ceded land. Fillmore found their arguments persuasive, and this, along with the Sandy Lake tragedy, compelled him to cancel the removal order.[4] After lawsuits brought by the Ojibwe and a series of federal court decisions in the 1980s and 1990s, the US Supreme Court ruled that the Ojibwe's right to hunt, fish, and gather on ceded lands had never been rescinded.

In the late nineteenth century, white expansion enveloped and overwhelmed the western Indian Territory, ultimately reaching the Pacific coast and prompting wars and conflict with indigenous Great Plains and western Indians. As the US military eventually crushed the resistance, the government established additional reservations throughout the West. Native people attempted to maintain traditional ways on the reservations, but life was grim. Missionaries assigned to reservations aggressively pressured Indians to abandon traditional beliefs. Cut off from traditional means of making a living, the people had to rely on the federal government for goods, services, and even food. The people were reduced to extreme poverty, and many reservations resembled refugee camps. Some progressive bureaucrats and religious societies were appalled at these conditions and sought to relieve them by advocating policies to greatly hasten assimilation into broader American society for the Indians' own good. At the same time, the American government began to view reservations as expensive obstacles to assimilation of Indian people and the lands themselves as necessary for American settlement.

The Great Suppression

The forced-assimilation era in American Indian policy lasted from the late 1870s to the early 1930s. More strenuous efforts—called the Great Suppression by some modern Native people—were made by missionaries assigned to reservations to convert the Indian people to

Figure 2.1

Indian boarding school at Lac du Flambeau Ojibwe Reservation, circa 1929 | WHi Image ID 35888

Christianity, and this was greatly supported by reservation agents who banned all "pagan" rituals. Missionaries had long operated mission schools on reservations, but beginning in the late 1870s, children were taken from their parents and sent to government boarding schools to learn the English language, the Christian faith, and menial work skills so that they could make a living in an American world (Figure 2.1). The speaking of Native languages was prohibited and punished in the schools.

In Wisconsin, government boarding schools were established at the Lac du Flambeau Ojibwe Reservation and the Oneida Reservation and in conjunction with Christian missions at the Bad River Ojibwe Reservation and the Menominee Reservation. Some children were sent to schools in other states.[5] The government also established multitribal schools in Hayward and Tomah; the school in Tomah drew many Ho-Chunk because of its proximity to Ho-Chunk settlements.

In an effort to replace a communal worldview with the concept of private ownership of land, the Dawes Act of 1887 divided reservations into parcels of land allotted to enrolled tribal members. The idea was to transform Native people into independent farmers and thus "sever tribal ties in favor of personal gain," in the words of noted anthropologist and historian Nancy Lurie. This would provide a path to "civilization."[6] Heads of families received 160-acre allotments, single people over the age of eighteen and minor orphans received 80 acres, and single people under eighteen received 40 acres. The allotments would be held in trust by the government, tax free, for twenty-five years, after which complete ownership of the lands would be granted. Many problems attended this plan, not the least of which was the way it conflicted with the egalitarian and communal ethics that were generally the nature of Native societies. Other problems doomed the plan to failure as well. To begin with, much of the land was of poor quality, ill-suited to farming. In addition, for many Native peoples farming was traditionally the role of women, and thus the transition was difficult for men to accept. Some tribes were unwilling to turn to farming as an alternative to previous modes of making a living and traditional forms of subsistence, including hunting and gathering over larger territory. Most Native people lacked farming equipment and resources and were uncertain how and when to pay the property taxes eventually assessed on the lands. In the end, many chose instead to rent out their allotments for income and eventually sold them to their non-Native neighbors in order to survive. Ownership itself became an issue over time, as descendants often found themselves one of several co-owners of a single allotment.[7]

In 1924, the United States extended citizenship to all Native people, ostensibly to honor the many Indian soldiers who volunteered and died in World War I. But this also seemed to many to be "simply another effort to diminish their tribal sovereignty and treaty rights."[8]

Ultimately, the policies of forced assimilation only exacerbated the suffering and deepened the poverty of Indian people, so much so that once again federal Indian policy had to be changed in the 1930s on humanitarian grounds—but not before great damage had been done. Many Native languages had been replaced by English, and many traditional customs and ceremonies had disappeared or been greatly eroded. In many cases individual tribes lost one-half to three-quarters of the land originally reserved for them by treaties—more than 150 million acres in all.[9] But Native cultures doggedly persisted, and in the 1920s many non-Indian people and the Department of the Interior itself began to recognize the cruelty, injustice, and even the ultimate futility of forced assimilation policies.

In 1928, the Meriam Report (officially titled "The Problem with Indian Administration") called for sweeping reforms, and subsequently the Indian Reorganization Act of 1934, introduced during the Roosevelt administration, offered a "New Deal" for Indians by canceling the policies and programs that had proved so harmful. In their place, the New Deal offered federally recognized Native nations a greater opportunity to manage their own affairs. They were allowed to reorganize by making their own constitutions and forming tribal governments modeled on the American style of democratic governance, with elected decision-making officials in contrast to traditional consensus-based tribal councils.

However, even this did not solve the "Indian problem" in the eyes of the federal government, and thus there would be other shifts in federal Indian policy during the twentieth century that would greatly affect Native people.[10] Current federal policy, termed "self-determination," reaffirms sovereign nation status of the tribes and allows Indian people to directly oversee federal programs on reservations. Even given that direction, tensions are once again growing as individual states, including Wisconsin, seek more political power over Indian nations within their borders in matters concerning environmental issues, treaty rights, and Indian gaming and casinos.

The Potawatomi and Their Neighbors

Drum Dance ceremonial communities like Skunk Hill were founded by Potawatomi people who had been greatly affected by long and early contact with the European and American policies of the nineteenth century. Originating in central Michigan, the Potawatomi are closely related to the Ojibwe and Ottawa, with whom they share similar customs and languages. By tradition, these three tribes formed an alliance called the Council of the Three Fires, each tribe having a distinctive cultural role. The Ojibwe are keepers of sacred scrolls and knowledge of the *Midewiwin*, or Grand Medicine Society; the Ottawa, keepers of trade; and the Potawatomi, keepers of the sacred fire, which can be viewed as a metaphor for the maintenance of traditional culture.[11]

Attacks by the eastern Iroquois, who desired to control the fur trade between Europeans and Indians, pushed the Potawatomi farther west and, in the early nineteenth century, eight thousand to ten thousand Potawatomi occupied a large territory covering what is now southern Michigan, northern Indiana, northeastern Illinois, and eastern Wisconsin. Here they lived in more than one hundred small villages and made a living from hunting, fishing, gathering wild plants, and growing corn and other crops. Social structure formed around kinship ties such as the clan system, consisting originally of as many as twenty-three clans.[12] Each community had a leader, or "chief," assisted by a council of adult males. There was no single ruler, but some chiefs attained more influence and power in broader Potawatomi affairs.

The Potawatomi had been active participants in the European and American fur trade, exchanging beaver and other pelts for manufactured trade goods that eventually replaced many traditional technologies and material culture and had now become critical for survival. Involvement in the fur trade also had consequences in the political sphere, as those successive traders, often the offspring of marriages between Potawatomi women and French traders, attained more political influence over traditional leadership.[13]

As the fur trade industry began to collapse in the 1820s and 1830s, Native people were deprived of much of their livelihood and the manufactured goods that were now necessities. As whites began to move in greater numbers to the frontiers of what would become the midwestern states, economic disparity and a thirst for land created

Figure 2.2

Illinois Potawatomi Chief Waubaunsee was among the signers of treaties that ceded lands. Americans, like Europeans before them, gifted prominent chiefs with military-style coats and medals bearing the images of American and European leaders.

| Lithograph from Thomas McKenney and James Hall, *The History of Indian Tribes of North America*, 3 vols. (Philadelphia: E. C. Biddle, 1838–1844); WHi Image ID 23927

a great deal of friction. In previous years, the Potawatomi and Ho-Chunk (then generally referred to as Winnebago) had ceded some lands for American use (Figures 2.2 and 2.3), but the Black Hawk War of 1832 in Illinois and Wisconsin provided the impetus for removal from virtually all of their remaining lands.[14] In that year, the Sauk leader Black Hawk led a large band of Sauk, Fox, and others across the Mississippi from Iowa to Illinois to reclaim lands lost in an earlier and controversial treaty. Black Hawk thought he could end

Figure 2.3

Indiana Potawatomi Chief Metea spoke against land cessions during 1821 treaty negotiations.
 Lithograph from Thomas McKenney and James Hall, *The History of Indian Tribes of North America*, 3 vols. (Philadelphia: E. C. Biddle, 1838–1844); WHi Image ID 113197

the conflict peacefully, but he also had been made to believe that if trouble ensued, he would have the support of the British and of other tribes. Black Hawk was further emboldened by visions of his spiritual adviser White Cloud, the Winnebago Prophet, who foresaw success in reclaiming lands, as well as by his own medicine bag, which he perceived as a powerful supernatural protector of the Sauk people.[15]

But resettlement was doomed from the start. It was aggressively opposed by the American military, the support from the British that Black Hawk expected never materialized, and neighboring tribes chose to formally stay out of the conflict, providing little support for Black Hawk's venture. US military, as well as state and territorial militia, chased Black Hawk and his large band north into Wisconsin, at the time part of Michigan Territory, engaging in skirmishes and battles and rebuffing diplomatic attempts on Black Hawk's part to stop the conflict. The conflict ended August 2–3, 1832, with the massacre of hundreds of Black Hawk's band near the confluence of the Bad Axe and Mississippi Rivers.

Despite the reprehensible massacre, the government viewed the conflict as another example of how Natives and whites could not be expected to peacefully coexist in the same region, and it was the Indians who had to go. Certainly, Black Hawk's audacious attempt to reclaim lands had drawn the sympathy of some of the Wisconsin Ho-Chunk and Potawatomi, but most had chosen to stay out of the conflict. Nevertheless, all people from both tribes would face the consequences. Within months of the conclusion of the Black Hawk War, the two tribes were being pressured to give up their lands and move west.

By the authority of several treaties in 1832 and 1837, many Ho-Chunk were forced to move to reservations—first in Minnesota, then in South Dakota, and finally in Nebraska, where the reservation of the Winnebago Tribe of Nebraska was established.[16] The Treaty of Chicago, signed in 1833, forced the Potawatomi of Wisconsin, northeastern Illinois, and Indiana onto lands in Iowa and then to the Kaw River in what would later become Kansas, where the Prairie Band Potawatomi Reservation was started[17] (Figure 2.4). Much later a Christian Potawatomi band broke off and established its own reservation in Oklahoma. Today they are known as the Citizens Band because, as Christians, they were extended US citizenship long before other Native Americans were given that status in 1924.

The Ojibwe and Menominee of Wisconsin escaped removals for various reasons, including their own diplomatic efforts and, for the Ojibwe, as a consequence of the disastrous attempt to remove them to Minnesota in 1850 that embarrassed the federal government. Their northern and forested territories were also less desirable for farming

Figure 2.4

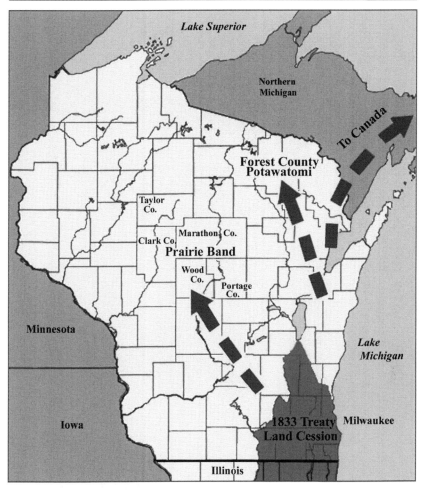

This map shows the remaining Potawatomi territory ceded in 1833 and the routes taken by those who resisted removal. | Robert Birmingham

and white settlement. Instead, various bands of Ojibwe retained small reservations in their homelands by an 1854 treaty, and another treaty signed in the same year provided a reservation for the Menominee within their once-extensive lands in northeastern Wisconsin.[18]

The 1833 treaty gave the Potawatomi people several years to move, and some found their way west. One band of Christian and other Potawatomi in Indiana was rounded up in 1838 and taken to the

Figure 2.5

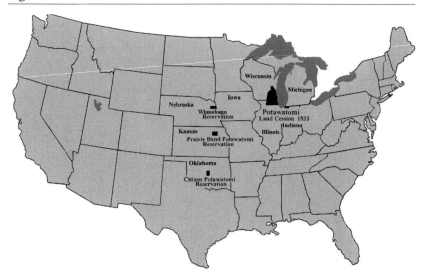

The locations of Potawatomi and Nebraska Winnebago reservations today | Robert Birmingham

western reservation under military escort. At least forty-two of them, mostly children, died of typhoid and exhaustion.[19] Others escaped along the route (Figure 2.5). Similar suffering attended the removals of Ho-Chunk, some of whom, in later removals, were herded into boxcars for transportation west,[20] painfully reminiscent of the removals of European Jews to concentration camps by the Nazis.

But many Ho-Chunk and Potawatomi resisted removal and lived as virtual refugees on their former lands, moving from place to place as increasing white settlement forced them into remoter areas. The displaced people of both tribes derived their living from a mixture of traditional pursuits supplemented by incomes from seasonal jobs in commercial enterprises, such as berry-picking operations and logging. The federal government made several attempts to round up the resisters, but these proved unsuccessful; those taken to the reservations simply kept slipping back to Wisconsin. Although they were allowed to return in the 1870s, the Ho-Chunk lived in scattered lands throughout the late nineteenth and early twentieth centuries. Some claimed homesteads under the Indian Homestead Act of 1881, but after a time most of these lands were lost because of property tax liabilities.[21] They did not seek formal recognition as a tribe by the federal government separate from their Nebraska Winnebago relatives until 1966, beginning with a single forty-acre homestead that had been held in trust by the federal government. They now form the Ho-Chunk Nation, with headquarters at Black River Falls, although their lands are scattered through several Wisconsin counties.

After the removals of the Potawatomi in the 1830s, bands of Potawatomi removal resisters gradually moved away from their former villages in eastern Wisconsin in two main directions. One group moved ever northward into the forests of northern Wisconsin, northern Michigan, and Canada. In Wisconsin this group settled on scattered lands. Wrote one Indian agent in 1907:

> These Indians have as rule no fixed homes, but roam place to place, picking berries, digging ginseng and other roots, working in logging camps etc. A few have homesteaded and now hold 40 to 80 acres of land, and have small clearings and erected log houses. In the main they are squatters and have built shelters and shacks and made small clearings in the forest or wherever vacant land could be found.[22]

Homesteads claimed by these Potawatomi under the Indian Reorganization Act formed the basis of the Forest County Potawatomi, federally recognized as a tribe in 1913.

Others gradually moved northwest to central Wisconsin near Ho-Chunk settlements, and this group in particular maintained close contact with their western Prairie Band Potawatomi relatives through frequent visits—so close that they became enrolled members of the reservation but were enumerated as absentees "living in Wisconsin."[23] Unhappy with reservation life, several hundred of those who had been removed left the reservation beginning in the 1860s to "live a more

Figure 2.6

This scene of the Indiana Potawatomi removal in 1838 was sketched by an eyewitness, George Winter.
| Tippecanoe County Historical Association

primitive life," as one Indian agent put it, with their central Wisconsin kin, now also referred to as Prairie Band Potawatomi[24] (Figure 2.6). There were some attempts to return the absentees to the reservation, but once again, they kept coming back to Wisconsin.

Relations with whites were mostly peaceful, but concerns arose about the rapidly diminishing game supply and, in 1871, rumors spread of a region-wide Indian uprising.[25] The US government developed a plan to return all of the "stray bands" of Potawatomi, Ho-Chunk, and Ojibwe in Wisconsin to their appropriate reservations, and Congress went so far as to appropriate funds for military action. This did not materialize, and, as the commissioner of Indian affairs observed, the plan wouldn't have worked in any case, since the Indians would only drift back as they had done before.[26]

The migration back to Wisconsin increased after 1880, simultaneous with the institution of the forced-assimilation policies on the reservation and the formation of the off-reservation Drum Dance communities. The returnees associated, lived, and intermarried with Ojibwe, Ho-Chunk, and other Potawatomi. As enrolled members of

the Prairie Band Potowatomi reservation, the Wisconsin absentees took an active interest in tribal affairs during lengthy visits back to Kansas, much to the dismay of reservation officials who, intent on making their charges industrious, viewed the visiting an enormous waste of time and money. They also characterized the Wisconsin people as "troublesome and insubordinate" and therefore a bad influence, no doubt because they clung to traditional ways.[27] Wisconsin Prairie Band people also received allotments on the reservation after 1887 when the Dawes Act was passed into law. Many rented out and possibly even sold the allotments to white farmers and ranchers to sustain their lives in Wisconsin. Ironically, the same policies meant to erode Native culture worked to reinforce Indian identity and traditions among the Prairie Band Potawatomi of Wisconsin. By 1918, approximately three hundred tribal members had returned from the Prairie Band Potawatomi reservation to Wisconsin, many living at Skunk Hill and its sister ceremonial community at McCord.[28]

3

New Hope: The Drum Dance

SOMEWHERE ON THE EASTERN Great Plains in the late nineteenth century, a Sioux woman or girl fled her village during an attack by enemies. She hid among the reeds of a marshy place for several days, during which the Great Spirit came to her in dreams and gave her instructions for a new way of life that would bring peace and hope to Indian people. She was to make a special large drum and instruct Indian people how to use it in ceremonies that included dancing and singing—the traditional forms of praying and offering thanks for blessings. The ceremonials would emphasize a moral code that rejected alcohol, gambling, and other vices. The new practice would bring the various Native peoples together in peace, and the whites would take notice of this and would be encouraged to pursue peaceful relations with Indians. The woman walked from village to village preaching this message, and the Drum passed from tribe to tribe.

This is the essence of the origin story of the Drum Dance found in slightly different versions passed down in oral histories of ceremonial societies among various tribes of the upper Midwest and Great Plains.[1] It is believed to have first appeared in the 1870s, and indeed, many oral traditions and historical documents identify the visionary as Wananikwe, or Tail Feather Woman, a Santee Sioux woman or girl living in western Minnesota. It is commonly related that the attack on her village was by the US Army, but the specific military action involved is unclear. Intertribal warfare may also have been involved.

Many Drum traditions state that the Sioux gave the Ojibwe an instrument of peace to stop the long-running and bloody conflict between the two tribes.[2] Citing alarmed letters by Indian agent E. Stephens from the Menominee Reservation concerning the "Sioux Dance" introduced there in 1881, one scholar, James Clifton, painted a darker picture, depicting the Drum Dance as anti-white and anti-Christian Indian.[3] However, such hostile sentiments are not a part of the Drum Dance traditions and in fact are antithetical to its message. If indeed this was the Drum Dance, as its timing suggests it was, the Indian agents probably misunderstood the peaceful intentions of the ceremonial and, fearing that it signaled a general uprising, cast it as a threat. Some settlers in Wisconsin had done the same when the Drum Dance was introduced there a few years earlier, in 1878.

It is also probable that the Drum Dance was confused with another messianic ceremonial, the Ghost Dance, which originated in Nevada after 1869 and later swept the Great Plains. The Ghost Dance taught that, through the dance rituals, whites and Christian Indians would be made to disappear. The interpreter and northern Wisconsin resident Benjamin Armstrong claimed in his memoirs to have met Tail Father Woman in 1878, but he mistakenly called her new ceremonial the Ghost Dance.[4] In reality, the Ghost Dance had little influence on the more easterly midwestern tribes.

The Drum Dance and Its Way of Life

At the heart of the Drum Dance ceremonials was the large Drum itself, a sacred object that is considered to be representative of the world and the powers of the Great Spirit and that is drummed by multiple individuals, reinforcing the concept of brotherhood. This departed from most previous customs where small hand drums accompanied singing and dancing. The concept of a large drum with multiple drummers is believed to have been a cultural borrowing from the older Grass Dance associated with warrior societies of the northern Great Plains.[5] Some oral histories recall that a metal washtub with a deer skin stretched across the top formed the first Drum, but quickly it became more elaborate, with a wooden frame and a painted head suspended by four feathered, crooked-staff legs.[6] Paint divided the head into fields of blue and red, with a yellow stripe running down the center, sometimes paralleled by thinner stripes of red and blue. The colors are symbolic of sacred cardinal directions: blue for north, red for south, and the yellow stripe representing the east-west direction. Decorations added to the upper edges of the Drum and a skirt included symbols that have great spiritual meaning to the makers and users, believed to depict spirit beings, symbols received in dreams, and figures representing the sun and the moon.[7]

The passing of the Drum and the accompanying ceremonial followed a protocol.[8] The Drum would be passed from individual to individual and between communities, with parts of an existing Drum used to make a new one. This was offered to a potential recipient along with ceremonies, songs, and the Drum Dance way of life. The person receiving the Drum would be deemed to be of good character and would have the means to be the keeper and guardian of the Drum itself. A great many gifts would be exchanged in the process. In this way, Drum Dance societies proliferated, sometimes with several among the same people. The Lac Courte Oreilles Ojibwe of Wisconsin had five Dream Dance societies in 1935, each at a principal settlement.[9] Further, any one society could receive several drums from other societies, and all of these would be used in turn during ceremonials. Reflecting its importance as a ceremonial community, Skunk Hill had four Drums under the care of the settlement's Drum Dance spiritual leader, John Nuwi.[10]

As a "pagan" ceremonial, the Drum Dance was technically illegal on reservations during the years of forced assimilation until the 1930s, but this seems to have been variously enforced. Some societies were able to more or less conduct the ceremonies openly, as apparently was done on the Lac Courte Oreilles Ojibwe Reservation and described by Samuel Barrett, a Milwaukee Public Museum anthropologist.[11] Others had to keep a low profile or held the ceremonials in secret. In some cases the Drum Dance was harshly oppressed by reservation officials, missionaries, or Christian converts.[12] At the Mille Lacs Ojibwe Reservation in Minnesota, missionaries drove ceremonies indoors where they could not be seen, and the dates of the ceremonies were kept secret. Writing in 1942, anthropologist John Gillin cited oral history stating that at some point tribal police stopped a dance held at the Lac du Flambeau Ojibwe Reservation in Wisconsin and told the dancers that "the government didn't permit Indian religion in this country."[13] Viewing ceremonial dancing as a threat to assimilation, the commissioner of Indian affairs went so far as to ban Indian dancing on reservations in 1923, one of the religious freedom outrages that led to the cancellation of forced-assimilation policies in 1934.[14]

The off-reservation Prairie Band Potawatomi living in Wisconsin had no such restrictions. In the decades before the founding of Skunk Hill, several ceremonial communities had already formed on unwanted or unused lands, away from the watchful eyes of reservation officials and missionaries, although pressure from white settlement resulted in a series of relocations. One former resident of the McCord ceremonial community in northern Wisconsin wrote that it offered a place "where many disenchanted and disempowered people from the Midewiwin and Big Drum began to gather a village setting."[15]

As practiced in the late nineteenth and early twentieth centuries, the main Drum Dance ceremonial itself was held several times a year in a specially constructed dance circle surrounded by a wood railing or fence, as at Skunk Hill (Figure 3.1), or sometimes in a rectangular

Figure 3.1

This undated postcard shows non-Indian visitors near a dance ring at Skunk Hill | Courtesy of Lester Public Library of Arpin, Powers Bluff file donated by Fred and Germaine Pigeon

dance enclosure. In some cases, an octagonal log structure referred to as a Round House served as a ceremonial space during inclement weather. Ceremonial, or "medicine," poles were erected at the dance grounds and often left in place.[16] At Skunk Hill, a high tree stripped of some lower branches served as a living ceremonial pole and remained in the former village at Powers Bluff for several decades, until decay forced its removal.

The raising of an American flag began ceremonies, and the common interpretation is that the flag represented the peace and protection promised by the American government and the guarantee of the religious freedom under the Constitution.[17] The ceremonials themselves started with a recounting of the origin of the Drum Dance, followed by four days of dance and songs accompanied by the Drum, as well as feasts, oratory, and gift exchanges. At various times, groups of men danced around the Drum while a group of women sang from the edge of the ceremonial space.

As an all-encompassing way of life, the Drum Dance also incorporated traditional rituals that served the many needs of the community, such as those associated with mourning.[18] The ceremonial was considered sacred, and generally onlookers not involved with the Drum were prohibited until the afternoon of the fourth day, when the general public was invited to observe, again emphasizing the concept of goodwill among peoples. Anthropologist Samuel Barrett was allowed to observe and even photograph many of the activities during one ceremonial at the Lac Courte Oreilles Ojibwe Reservation in 1910.[19]

Cultural Revitalization

The Drum Dance was among several, and among the most successful, cultural or nativistic revitalization movements that appeared among Native peoples in the nineteenth century as traditional ways began to slip away due to pressures and influence from suppressive US policy. Now known as the Big Drum, such societies remain active on many midwestern and eastern Great Plains reservations, and in some communities off-reservation, notably among the Prairie Band Potawatomi descendants of Skunk Hill living near Wisconsin Rapids, Wisconsin.

Revitalization movements occur the world over and are typically introduced by prophets, dreamers, or visionaries who preach new ways to deal with the stresses caused by rapid change or cultural suppression, but also with an emphasis on restoring traditional customs and values.[20] These are often referred to as religions, as was the case with the Drum Dance, but this is a misnomer in the case of North American Native people. On the contrary, Native views of what elsewhere are called religions are perceived as a way of life that permeates all human activity.

Some of the movements, like the Drum Dance, emphasized peace among Native and non-Native peoples, and they helped reconcile changing life with traditional Native values. In the example of the Longhouse or Handsome Lake practice among the Iroquois, the visions of prophet Handsome Lake blended tradition with Christian principles and deities and remains today an accepted way of life among the Iroquois.[21] As well, in the first decade of the twentieth century some Ho-Chunk in Nebraska and Wisconsin adopted the pan-tribal Peyote Religion (or Native American Church, as it is formally known), which incorporates Christian theology into traditional beliefs and includes taking the hallucinogen peyote as a sacrament to induce visions. Peyote grows in Texas and Mexico, and the rites originated in the southern Great Plains of the United States.[22] It too remains active.

Others took on a more revolutionary form, seeking no less than total rejection of white ways and expulsion of the whites themselves. Following the dreams and visions of his brother, the Shawnee prophet Tenskwatawa, Tecumseh of the Ohio River valley led an intertribal movement to resist white incursions into the frontier during the years 1810 to 1813.[23] The teachings of Tenskwatawa and Tecumseh reached as far west as present-day Wisconsin, where Potawatomi and others joined the movement. The Ojibwe living on Chequamegon Bay in Lake Superior, in the northern reaches of what is now Wisconsin, are said to have briefly abandoned their other traditions, throwing their sacred bags into Lake Superior.[24] Viewing Tecumseh as a powerful ally against the Americans, the British supported Tecumseh, and his war became a part of the War of 1812 when his warriors helped take key American military posts. The Americans ultimately crushed the rebellion, killing Tecumseh.

The most famous nativistic or revitalization movement, the Ghost Dance, swept across the Great Plains as wars continued with the US Army, who sought to confine Natives to reservations and eliminate Indian cultures and traditions.[25] Beginning around 1869 among the Paiute of Nevada, and further enhanced and strengthened by the Paiute prophet Wovoka in 1889, the Ghost Dance incorporated dancing and singing with a message of peace, hope, and the return of the good life for Native people. As it spread, it emphasized an apocalyptic vision whereby dead friends and relatives would return and the whites would magically disappear. Ghost Dance warriors became emboldened by the belief that special shirts would make them impervious to bullets. The US government viewed the Ghost Dance as an uprising and suppressed it by military action. Its widespread practice on the Great Plains effectively ended with the massacre by the US Army of several hundred Sioux Ghost Dancers and their children under the leadership of Big Foot at Wounded Knee, South Dakota, on December 29, 1890, as the group was being escorted to a reservation.[26]

Unlike the Great Plains Ghost Dance, the Drum Dance spread east to midwestern tribes that were not at war with the US government at the time but nevertheless found attractive its message of hope, peace, and cultural persistence during a time of government-sponsored suppression.

4

The Spread of the Drum Dance

Beginning in the 1870s with the Santee Sioux in Minnesota, the ceremonies and lifestyle of the Drum Dance were passed from tribe to tribe over many decades, with ceremonial societies starting both on and off reservations. In the late 1870s, the Santee Sioux passed the Drum to the more easterly Ojibwe in Minnesota and Wisconsin. The Wisconsin Ojibwe accepted the ceremonial in 1878 along the St. Croix River on the Wisconsin–Minnesota border (Figure 4.1), causing alarm among white settlers. In that year, loud drumming suddenly

Figure 4.1

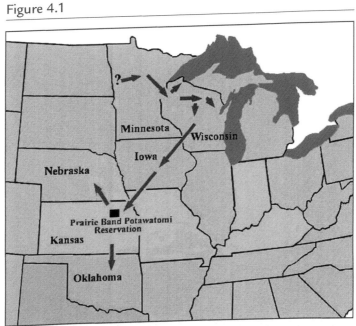

The spread of the Drum Dance | Robert Birmingham

33

erupted from villages of the St. Croix Band of Ojibwe who lived in scattered settlements throughout the area. Fearing it was a precursor to war, settlers called on the US Army to investigate and put down the feared uprising. Concerns quickly dissipated as the military officers discovered the peaceful nature of the ceremonials, and the episode has come down in history as the Wisconsin Scare of 1878.[1]

That same year, the St. Croix Ojibwe passed the ceremonial to other Ojibwe living in Wisconsin as recorded in the autobiographical letters of Eliza Morrison, a woman of mixed Ojibwe and European ancestry born on Madeline Island in Lake Superior. Morrison, who lived in northwestern Wisconsin with her Scotland-born husband, recounted that in 1878, twenty people from the mouth of the Yellow River at its confluence with the St. Croix River (Danbury, Wisconsin) stopped at her family residence on their way to bring the Drum to the Bad River Ojibwe on Chequamegon Bay in Lake Superior. The group included one woman, a recent widow of a medicine man, who may or may not have been Tail Feather Woman herself.[2] Wisconsin resident Benjamin Armstrong, who claimed to have met Tail Feather Woman on the south shore of Lake Superior in 1878, described her as a young girl; however, this claim has been disputed by modern scholarship.[3]

From the Ojibwe, the Drum and the message of the Sioux prophet passed in the early 1880s to the Menominee Reservation in northeast Wisconsin and to the off-reservation Prairie Band Potawatomi living in central Wisconsin. In a circular fashion, the absentee Wisconsin Prairie Band Potawatomi would take the Drum Dance back west to the Kansas reservation in 1884. In 1888, the Ojibwe introduced Drum Dance Drums and accompanying teachings to the Wisconsin Ho-Chunk, but the Ho-Chunk subsequently incorporated only the ornate Drum into their own traditional dances.[4]

John Young and the Drum Dance

A key figure in the promotion and spread of the Drum Dance among the Prairie Band Potawatomi was Wisconsin-born Nsowakwet, better known as John Young (Figure 4.2). Young was descended from those Potawatomi who had moved north from the Chicago area to south-

Figure 4.2

Studio portrait of John Young | WHi Image ID 33313

eastern Wisconsin in the early nineteenth century, later stopping in central Wisconsin to avoid removal. According to a short biography written by Albert Thunder, a frequent Ho-Chunk visitor to Skunk Hill, Young lived briefly at several places along the way to central Wisconsin but later lived with or near the Ho-Chunk near Pittsville, Wisconsin, who had similarly refused to be removed west.[5]

Like many other Potawatomi living in central Wisconsin, Young became enrolled as an "absentee" member of the Prairie Band Potawatomi Reservation, and like others, he maintained close contact with the Kansas reservation through regular visits, despite the great distance. On the reservation he was recognized as a councilman representing the interests of his Wisconsin tribal members. On behalf of the Wisconsin absentee people, he joined others living on the reservation to oppose the allotments under the Dawes Act of 1887. He resisted so vigorously that reservation Indian agents threatened to drop Young and other dissenting absentees from tribal roles or have them arrested if they did not move to the reservation.[6] Ultimately, Young and the others were assigned allotments despite the protestations. Sometime after 1878, Young became a disciple of the Drum Dance and headed a "stray band" that formed a succession of small communities in Wisconsin around the Drum and its way of life on unused or unwanted lands, moving his villages ever north into more and more remote parts of Wisconsin.

The Big Eau Pleine Ceremonial Community

Thunder wrote that John Young moved briefly to Skunk Hill after settling in central Wisconsin, so it is possible that the first Potawatomi Drum Dance ceremonials were held here. However, the first well documented of his ceremonial communities, dating from the 1880s to 1890s, was located along the Big Eau Pleine River about four miles from the small settlement of Rozellville (Marathon County), established in 1876[7] (Figure 4.3). As with Native American villages stretching back to antiquity, Young's community was well situated at a natural ford of a river with major springs that provided fresh water year-round. This area provided food and resources from which Native people derived a stable and comfortable subsistence. Here Young's band grew potatoes, corn, beans, squash, and onions. Meat was provided by deer and muskrat and fish. In the warmer months, the residents drew income from picking blueberries and cranberries. Because the Indians grew crops, the settlers referred to the Indian settlement as Indian Farms.[8]

Figure 4.3

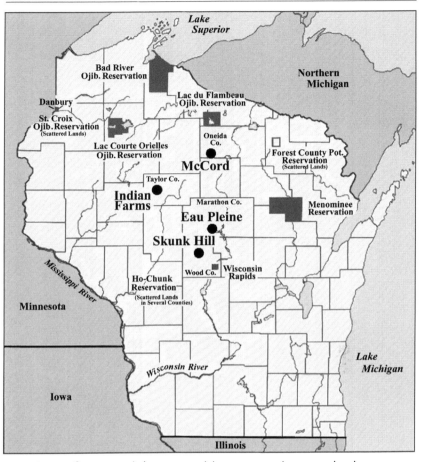

Locations of ceremonial communities, reservations, and other places mentioned in text | Robert Birmingham

Also like Potawatomi ceremonial communities, including Skunk Hill, stands of sugar maple were a prominent environmental feature. From these trees sap could be obtained in spring and boiled into maple sugar syrup that could be consumed but also sold to settlers. Another Indian name for the Big Eau Pleine River translates as "Soft Maple River."[9] Maple sugaring was an important activity to all Native peoples of the north; not only was it a sweet food source that also had commercial value, it also was cause for a major social event that reconnected families for about a month after the harsh winter as they assembled in their "sugar bushes." An important ceremonial that drew many visitors to Indian Farms was the Sugar Dance, which welcomed spring and the flow of sugar maple sap.

An active trade and cordial relations developed between Young's band and Rozellville residents. The Indian people traded pelts, venison, ginseng, maple sugar, cranberries and other berries, and slippery elm bark, for which they obtained cash or goods. John Brinkman ran the general store and trading post where the trade was conducted, and, according to his daughter, the town at one time had become "Indian-oriented."[10] The settlers learned Potawatomi words and phrases to communicate with their non-English-speaking Indian neighbors.

Other cash income no doubt came from renting western reservation allotments to area ranchers and farmers with the assistance of Indian agents. John Young held an allotment, as did John Nuwi, another Wisconsin Drum Dance principal who would later live at Skunk Hill. However, even before the 1886 allotments, Marathon County records from 1882 show that one John Young from Kansas owned property next to John Brinkman's and elsewhere near Rozellville, perhaps with the intention of forming a land base for the band.[11]

Two separate villages composed the larger Big Eau Pleine/ Indian Farms Drum Dance community, where about 130 people lived in log cabins or traditional bark- or mat-covered lodges. One was a Potawatomi village, headed by John Young, and the other, about a mile away, accommodated Wisconsin Ojibwe Dream Dance devotees headed by Paul Whitefish (Figure 4.4). Whitefish had married a Potawatomi woman and

Figure 4.4

Paul Whitefish and family |

Photo from *Westboro, 1875–1975: Pages of History*, by G. Hill, G. J. Biersack, V. Thums, P. Ochodnicky, and J. Spieles, 1975, 59. Reprinted by permission of Roy Speils. Copy available at Westboro (Wisconsin) Public Library.

probably came from the Lac Courte Oreilles Reservation. A large, railed dance circle at Young's village formed the central ceremonial structure, and, according to the reminiscences of white settlers, the seasonal ceremonies became a "rendezvous for all Indians," including large numbers who traveled from the western reservation.[12]

Despite good relations with white settlers, the Indians did not formally own the land, and so increasing settlement pressures forced Young and his followers farther north by the end of the nineteenth century. One old story related that a settler named Saunders bought the property where Young's village was located and gave the Indians some cash to move on. When some did not leave, he burned their houses.[13]

The Drum Dance on the Potowatomi Reservation

Back on the Great Plains Prairie Band Potawatomi reservation, life had grown harder under the policies of forced assimilation, with its prohibition of Native religion and language, the establishment of boarding schools, and allotments of communally owned land. Many embraced the Native-oriented, hopeful message of the Drum Dance brought to them in 1884 during a visit from John Young and the Wisconsin Prairie Band Potawatomi. At first even the reservation authorities noted some positive aspects to the ceremonials and teachings:

> There has been introduced into the Pottawatomie tribe in the past year a system of worship which consists principally of dancing and exulting, though, like all semi-civilized nations, clouded in superstition. Apart from the superstition and consumption of time spent in those dances, the moral tendency is very good, as the teaching is in accordance with the Ten Commandments. They object to sacrament by the use of intoxicating drink, and denounce gambling and horse racing.[14]

Although the ceremonies were technically forbidden, Indian agents therefore felt reluctant to interfere with them; however, they discouraged frequent "meetings" for the ceremonials.[15] At the same time, the agents viewed the Wisconsin Potawatomi as "troublesome and insubordinate," because of their opposition to allotments as well as their influence promoting Native ways.[16]

Indian Farms, Taylor County

By the late 1890s, Young and Whitefish sought a remoter place to practice the Drum Dance way of life, moving to an abandoned logging camp on the Little Yellow River in Taylor County, Wisconsin.[17] The recently logged-over lands provided a habitat for deer, and a major road led to area towns where some necessities could be obtained by cash or barter. This place was also known as Indian Farms, because residents kept gardens where they raised crops.

Newspapers tracked the Native people's northward migration from the Big Eau Pleine to the Little Yellow River during the years 1896 and 1897, as well as the excitement caused as groups of Indians with their ponies moved through the small towns, reporting that it was "a good opportunity for Kodaks."[18] The reaction to the presence of the Indians changed a bit when the whites learned of their intention to stay. A Taylor County newspaper reported that about one hundred Indians were camping on the Yellow River, killing deer and putting up hay for the winter for their horses. Worried about the impact on wild-life upon which the settlers also relied, the editors urged that Indian agents look into the matter, since the Indians did not belong to any reservation.[19] Later, a county warden arrested John Young for poaching deer, and he spent some time in jail before the fine was paid.[20]

Young and Whitefish maintained separate villages of log cabins about a half mile apart, and the Drum Dance continued to be the focus of community life. An earthen-banked dance ring forty feet in diameter is still visible on Chequamegon National Forest land and, as at the settlement at Big Eau Pleine, the new Indian Farms attracted many visitors and participants, including many from the Kansas reservation who came for the ceremonies. Also like the earlier settlement, people drew a livelihood from mixed traditional and cash economies, including trade with white settlers.

But tension once again arose when the Indians were accused of stealing horses. It escalated greatly when an outbreak of smallpox hit Indian Farms during the years 1900–1901. According to some who lived nearby at the time, the disease may have killed over half of the estimated population of 130.[21] Settlers believed that the disease had been carried to the area by visiting Potawatomi from Kansas. However, the pox epidemic, one of the last in North America, was in fact widespread, and the warnings to get vaccinated had been previously published because of outbreaks elsewhere in Wisconsin as well as places like New York and Boston.[22] In any case, the irony is that Native people were blamed for bringing with them a disease that originated in Europe and that, since its introduction to the Americas in the late 1400s, had killed hundreds of thousands.

Taylor County health officials responded to the epidemic by putting the Indian settlement under quarantine, warning others not to allow the Indians into the towns. Guards were posted to keep the Indians away, and elsewhere in Wisconsin Ho-Chunk people were also quarantined.[23] The lack of medical care no doubt contributed to the high death toll reported by a Kansas Indian agent for the Wisconsin Prairie Potawatomi in 1901.[24]

A few years later, Young and many of his band were on the move again. Area residents later reported that many graves at Indian Farms were dug up in the 1930s by curiosity seekers and looters.

McCord

After Indian Farms, Young and his many followers moved even farther north into the marshes and dense forests of Oneida County, Wisconsin, which were in the process of regrowth after the end of the logging era. They settled in an abandoned logging camp where apparently some off-reservation Native people had already been living.[25] Today, this is still a remote area just a short distance from the modern vacation community of Tomahawk and about fifteen miles south of the Lac du Flambeau Ojibwe Reservation. The community bears the name of a tiny nearby settlement, McCord.

Figure 4.5

Studio portrait of John Young's daughter who married Kitchcumme of Skunk Hill; she is identified here as Mrs. Ketch-ka-mi (*sic*). | WHi Image ID 3608

Not all of Young's band followed, at least not on a permanent basis. Some, like John Nuwi, as well as some members of the Young family, became part of the new Drum Dance community at Skunk Hill in central Wisconsin. The two communities remained connected by the Drum Dance and kinship. John Young's daughter had lived on the Kansas reservation and moved to Skunk Hill with her Kansas-born husband, Kitchcumme (Figure 4.5). People moved between the two communities for ceremonies, often staying and visiting relatives for a considerable length of time. Some later moved to McCord from Skunk Hill as that community dwindled.

The McCord village was physically the largest of the Wisconsin Drum Dance communities, spreading over 440 acres of land along the Somo River and accommodating about ten families living in log cabins.[26] Prairie Band Potawatomi and Ojibwe from the Lac du Flambeau Reservation, who often intermarried, composed most of the population, but they were joined there by some Forest County Potawatomi, Menominee, and Ho-Chunk.[27]

The importance of the village as a ceremonial center is reflected by the structures erected there. Aside from log cabins used for homes, the McCord people maintained a characteristic Drum Dance ring, perhaps two, but also added a more elaborate octagonal dance hall (Figure 4.6). The rites of the Grand Medicine Society, or Midewiwin, were conducted in two lodges. The climate and soils in this part of Wisconsin were not particularly well suited for agriculture, but the residents planted gardens, hunted game, fished, took seasonal jobs,

Figure 4.6

Remains of the octagonal log dance hall at McCord | Photo courtesy of the Office of the State Archaeologist, Wisconsin Historical Society

and brought Native-made crafts and products like maple sugar to the market in the town of Tomahawk, six miles to the east.

After the turn of the twentieth century and especially with the development of the automobile, a summer vacation industry mushroomed around the many lakes of northern Wisconsin, drawing visitors from as far away as Illinois. During archaeological surveys of the McCord site in the 1990s done for the purpose of nominating it to the National Register of Historic Places, archaeologists from the Wisconsin Historical Society identified ten U-shaped stone and earthen-ridged foundations called boiling arches, seven to eleven feet long and two to three feet wide, many with central fireboxes and metal debris from supports for the boiling containers. These boiling arches were used for boiling sugar maple sap in iron pans to make maple sugar and syrup. According to Matthew Thomas, who did a study of the boiling arches, they comprise the largest concentration "of archaeological remains of boiling arches at an American Indian community in Wisconsin" and attest to the economic and social importance of maple syrup production at McCord.[28]

John Young died and was buried at McCord. The community continued to serve as a ceremonial center throughout the 1930s but thereafter lost most of its population as the Drum Dance declined. A few people lived there until the 1950s. The remains of the village are now preserved on Oneida County lands through the work of the Wisconsin Historical Society in consultation with area Natives and Oneida County. McCord was added to the National Register of Historic Places in 2000, and the National Park Service subsequently highlighted the history of McCord in 2001 as part of its Native American Heritage Month. Similar attention would be paid to sister ceremonial community Skunk Hill, founded by Drum Dance people who had left the western Prairie Band Potawatomi Reservation for Wisconsin in 1905.

5

The Skunk Hill Ceremonial Community

By THE OPENING YEARS of the twentieth century, Potawatomi on the Great Plains Prairie Band reservation faced many difficulties and much stress as a result of the forced-assimilation era. Thousands of acres of formerly communal land had passed out of their hands as a consequence of the Dawes Act, leading to general impoverishment, and those traditional people who refused to send their children to government schools were threatened with the loss of annuities and other payments.[1]

Initially tolerated by Indian agents on the reservation because of its good moral teachings, the Drum Dance in the 1890s became the focus of oppression. Reservation authorities now perceived it as an obstacle to assimilation and believed that the ceremonials were becoming like the much-feared Ghost Dance, which appeared to Americans as an uprising and had been recently suppressed by the US military. Indian agents now tried to break up the Drum Dance rituals with threat of military force.[2]

Disheartened with life in Kansas and seeking a safer place to pursue a traditional way of life, a number of Drum Dance members, other adults, and their families left the reservation and returned to Wisconsin, establishing the Skunk Hill community in 1905. There they joined relatives who were able to practice their religious beliefs and traditions without interference by government authorities. This move was made with the assent of Indian agents who were no doubt eager to get rid of troublemakers and further open reservation land to non-Indian, white farmers and ranchers. In fact, in 1919 the Kansas Potawatomi petitioned Indian agents to sell their allotments but were told they could do so only if they bought land in Wisconsin—an ironic reverse removal policy obviously meant to help dissolve the reservation.[3] Many Potawatomi did purchase land in Wisconsin for the new Skunk Hill community with proceeds from the rental of allotted land handled by the US government. A local newspaper reported that the Skunk Hill residents held a celebratory dance in October 1909 as the community received quarterly payments.[4] However, the selection of the land at Skunk Hill in Wood County, Wisconsin, seems to have been made by Potawatomi themselves, for the land had prior cultural and religious significance. As previously mentioned, John Young is said to have briefly lived on Skunk Hill shortly after migrating from southeastern Wisconsin and prior to the establishment of his ceremonial communities of Eau Pleine, Indian Farms, and McCord beginning in the 1880s. The Drum Dance may have been first held here among the Wisconsin Prairie Potawatomi after Young became a disciple of Tail Feather Woman sometime after 1878. One elder, Tom Kichkumme (grandson of Tom of the same last name, spelled differently), who lived at Skunk Hill as a child, tells a story passed down to him in which some people on the Kansas reservation had visions of Skunk Hill in Wisconsin "all lit up," showing that the Kansas people should move there. He said even today many good spirits live on the hill.[5]

The origin of the name Tah-qua-kik (or Skunk Hill, or Skunk Place) is unknown, but the name probably goes back to John Young's time in the area. One story is that it honored the homeland of many of the Prairie Band Potawatomi prior to removals around Chicago. The name *Chicago* derives from the Potawatomi word for "skunk," as related by John Nuwi, a resident of Skunk Hill and expert on Potawatomi place names in Illinois and Wisconsin; Nuwi told Alphonse Gerend that the word *Chicago* came from a Potawatomi story involving a skunk.[6] Another common interpretation is that the name for the city came from a type of wild garlic that grew along the Chicago River, for which the Potawatomi also used the word for skunk.

In any case, the prominence had already been known as Skunk Hill when the John Arpin Logging Company bought the land in 1889, establishing a logging camp and sawmill.[7] The loggers clear-cut the area of trees for lumber, leading to another name for the hill, Bald Mountain. The logging company closed its holdings in 1904, a year before the Potawatomi came to the hill from Kansas.[8] At what point in the nineteenth century the hill acquired the name Powers Bluff is uncertain, but it may have been named for a prominent Grand Rapids businessman and judge, Levi Parsons Powers.[9]

The Founding of the Skunk Hill Community

The city of Wisconsin Rapids, known as Grand Rapids until 1920, straddles the Wisconsin River in Wood County, Wisconsin. Like many of the river settlements in the northern and central parts of the state, it began in the mid-nineteenth century as a mill town for the lumber in-dustry. In 1905 it was surrounded by farms, vast wetlands, and smaller towns like Arpin, founded in 1890 by John Arpin.[10]

Native people who lived on the periphery of Grand Rapids and other towns, the displaced Potawatomi and Ho-Chunk, came to the towns to purchase goods and to sell hand-picked berries or to seek seasonal employment with the commercial lumber and berry indus-tries. The picking of various types of berries, including cranberries and blueberries, offered a major source of income for Indian people in central and northern Wisconsin during this period (Figure 5.1). Many

Figure 5.1

Ho-Chunk people and others harvest cranberries near Black River Falls, Wisconsin, circa 1900. | Photo by Charles van Schaick, WHi Image ID 63713

were employed as migrant workers, going place to place, often transported by trains.[11] Although the whites of the region looked down on Native people as uncivilized, the two groups long coexisted in the region without major conflicts.

Although the people of the region were familiar with the comings and goings of Native people, the rather new residents of Arpin were nevertheless surprised when a train pulled into the small depot in 1905 carrying a large number of Potawatomi people, including whole families, from the western Prairie Band Potawatomi reservation heading to Skunk Hill one mile away. Mary Day (1898–1984) told a newspaper correspondent of coming to Arpin from Kansas as a child with her grandfather, White Pigeon, and camping at the train depot (Figure 5.2). They built temporary bark wigwams on the hill and soon commenced construction of more permanent houses.[12]

At first local people questioned Indian ownership of the lands, but the Potawatomi insisted that the land had been set aside for them by the government.[13] Later it became evident that, in fact, legal purchases had been made in the names of Potawatomi people from

Figure 5.2

Early twentieth-century photo of the Arpin railroad depot | Courtesy of Lester Public Library of Arpin, Powers Bluff file donated by Fred and Germaine Pigeon

private landowners, although deeds seem to have not been formally recorded until a few years later. Up through the mid-1920s, land records in the form of deeds and entries on plat books that provided land ownership information show that Indian people would eventually own a total of 120 acres of land on the south side of Skunk Hill in ten- and twenty-acre parcels. In 1914, a ten-acre parcel on Skunk Hill went for $125. Over time, landowner names of these parcels included Sha-oh-nuk-dous, Sho-no-mo-quah, Shu-na-quoak, Mixequa and co-owner Keo-Komsquah, Squagishgoguah and co-owner Shohm, Cody Jackson, White Pigeon, Eagle Pigeon, Frank Young, and John Louie.[14] Some of the land appears to have passed among these landowners through time.

The spelling of Indian names was phonetic, leading to differences across documents, and so it is difficult to identify specific people for certain. Additionally, people sometimes had more than one Indian name, an English name, and even a nickname. However, a comparison of ownership records with the 1910 federal census that included Skunk Hill (see Appendix 1) indicates that Sha-oh-nuk-dous was most probably the Kansas-born Sho-no-kuk-doos recorded in the census, also known as longtime resident John Quatose (also spelled Kaudos); and Sho-no-mo-quah was Shea-na-yo-quah from Wisconsin, also known as Jim Spoon. Shu-na-quoak was probably Kansas-born She-no-quik in the census. Keo-Komsquah was almost certainly the Kansas-born Keo-kum-ma-qua in the census, and her co-owner in a parcel, Mixequa, was her widowed mother whose name appears as the similar-sounding Mek-sik-qua in the census record. Shohm was probably Wisconsin-born Sham in the census, and co-owner Squagishgoguah was his daughter Sueg-quish-kink-qua, also in the census. The name John Louie appears on deeds, and this is John Nuwi, Wisconsin Potawatomi and prominent Skunk Hill resident and founder, who was also known as John Louie or Louis. Identical or similar names of many of the landowners can also be found in the roll of allotment owners on the Kansas reservation and noted as "living in Wisconsin" as of 1918 (see Appendix 2).[15]

A Native Community

The general populace around Skunk Hill took a great interest in their new neighbors. For years area newspapers ran articles describing community events and ceremonies. Anthropologists and other scholars gathered information about the Skunk Hill community and its ceremonies because of its uniqueness and no doubt to document Native cultures that were perceived at the time to be rapidly vanishing. Among these visitors was Alphonse Gerend, a dentist from Sheboygan, Wisconsin, who later moved to Maine. Gerend developed an intense interest in Potawatomi culture and history, visiting Skunk Hill on numerous occasions beginning about 1909. He befriended the residents, who provided him with much information about the community and its history that he included in a long feature article he wrote for the *Sheboygan Press* newspaper in 1932 entitled "Traditions and Customs of the Once Powerful Indian Tribes That Roamed Over the State of Wisconsin."[16] In it he discussed the histories of the other ceremonial communities at Eau Pleine, Indian Farms in Taylor County, and Mc-Cord, gleaned from both his own studies and other sources. Along with his notes and papers, Gerend left behind a remarkable photographic record of the Skunk Hill community that is now curated at the Wisconsin Historical Society.[17]

Cordial relationships and even friendships developed with non-Indian neighbors as recalled by elderly area residents in interviews by myself and others during the years 1999 and 2000. Arpin native Norm Severt remembered that Joe Link, a bachelor from Skunk Hill, did odd jobs for his mother and became a frequent dinner guest at their home.[18] The family called him Uncle Joe. As a youth, Lyle Hamel lived on the family farm established in 1929 adjacent to the hill, and the people left at Skunk Hill at that time were their closest neighbors. He told me that White Pigeon, the elderly and mostly blind leader of the community, came to the house for visits and shared his personal stories.[19]

Figure 5.3

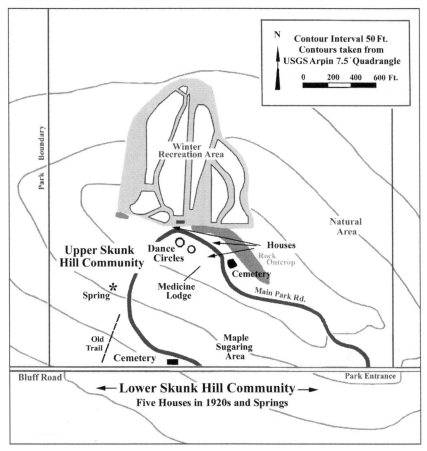

This map depicts the features of Skunk Hill circa 1920 along with modern-day park elements and roads. | Robert Birmingham

Layout of the Community

The Skunk Hill community was divided into two areas with a combination of log cabins, tar-papered structures, clapboard houses, and traditional bark lodges and wigwams (Figure 5.3). The main part of the village, consisting of about eight to ten structures, was arranged near the top of the hill against large outcrops of quartzite and around

Figure 5.4

Men and boys pose in front of houses at Skunk Hill. Some are dressed in ceremonial regalia. | Photo by Edith McKlem; WHi Image ID 113526

Figure 5.5

A wigwam stands next to a log cabin on top of Skunk Hill. Other houses can be seen in the distance. The wigwam could have been used for guest lodging or as a cooler summer residence.
| From the Carol Snowball Collection

Figure 5.6

A wooden
structure built
over a spring
and used for
obtaining water
| Alphonse Gerend
Photograph Album,
Wisconsin Historical
Society Archives; WHi
Image ID 113801

the dance rings used in Drum Dance ceremonials (Figures 5.4 and 5.5). The only source of water was a spring that flowed from the slope of the hill (Figure 5.6). According to Potawatomi elders, a large elm-bark structure near the dance ring was used for winter ceremonies, and the sacred Drums were apparently housed there or in another elm-bark structure.

Visitors came for varying lengths of time and often stayed in canvas tents, some of which are seen in period photographs. A small

Figure 5.7

Wood grave houses at Skunk Hill | Alphonse Gerend Photograph
Album, Wisconsin Historical Society Archives; WHi Image ID 113527

cemetery (now enclosed by a low rock wall) on the east side of the upper village served the community and was called the John Nee Wee (Nuwi) cemetery after the community cofounder was buried there in 1927. Graves had once been marked by customary Potawatomi structures consisting of small cut logs laid across the tomb and arranged in a low pyramidal shape or roofed wood-board structures also common among the Ojibwe (Figure 5.7). Before the building of some of the modern roads, a trail came from the west into the village and then headed down the steep north slope side of the hill that led to Arpin.

The community expanded over time to the much less rocky lower south slope, where larger and more substantial wood-frame and clapboard houses were eventually built (Figure 5.8). Water here also came from springs flowing from the hill. Potawatomi elders remembered those living below the main village late in its history as Frank Young, Frank Link, Eagle Pigeon, John Quatose or Kaudos (Sho-no-kuk-doos), and John Nuwi. Community residents established a second cemetery with traditional wood grave houses, now also enclosed by a rock wall, near the base of a rocky hill along the former lower part of

Figure 5.8

The house of the Frank Young family, in the lower part of the Skunk Hill community | From the Carol Snowball Collection

the village. It is called the Indian Bill cemetery, perhaps after medicine man Bill Spoon, whose probable Indian name, Shog-naab-ko-quak (spelled She-na-yo-qua in the 1910 census), appeared on one grave marker in 1936. Others buried there include Nek-sek, Mo-quan, and Me-Qus.[20]

This second cemetery, in deeper soil lower on the hill, was probably needed because of a lack of space around the upper one. The bedrock is very close to the surface at the top of the hill, a majestic outcropping at the crest, so there were very few places where excavations for graves could be made. The original wood grave houses also decayed over time, as is appropriate in Indian traditions. Some decades ago a park employee rebuilt the structures as wood-plank grave houses that have also mostly decayed since then.

Skunk Hill residents raised, collected, and hunted some of their own food, but much food and other supplies had to be obtained by cash and through barter. Powers Bluff is physically prominent and impressive, but it was actually not a very good place to establish a community in terms of sustainable natural resources; this emphasizes its role as a ceremonial community rather than one were a living could be made easily by traditional and self-sustaining methods. The existence of surrounding farms and towns would have made deer hunting difficult, if not impossible, and only small animals like squirrels, rabbits, and woodchucks could be found on the hill itself. Although residents planted gardens, the agricultural potential was poor over much of the hill because of the shallow, rocky soils, and the surrounding land was undesirable for area farmers.

However, much food and other necessary supplies could be purchased from stores in the towns of Arpin and Pittsville to the west, using cash obtained from government payments and through seasonal labor. Some members of the community no doubt found employment as pickers for area commercial berry operations. Elders recall that potato picking on farms in central Wisconsin brought additional income. Necessities were also acquired through barter and purchases with neighboring farms. The adjacent Hamel farm employed Skunk Hill villagers to help around the farm, and that family obtained some Native-made objects, including beadwork, in trade for other goods, such as milk

Figure 5.9

Lyle Hamel acquired this orange and black beaded neckband as a youth around 1930 from Skunk Hill boys in exchange for the use of his bicycle for a week. The band had reportedly belonged to White Pigeon, who died in 1931. In recent years, Lyle presented the neckband, along with a stone ceremonial pipe bowl, to Skunk Hill descendants. The central image is a butterfly with circle and cross symbols that are traditional Native American earth representations. The cross represents the four sacred directions. Adjacent are forktailed birds (possibly swallows); the object in their beaks might be branches, reminiscent of the common dove with olive branch peace motif, or perhaps a worm, representing the cyclical rebirth of nature and the world celebrated in spring by Native people. | From the author's collection; photo courtesy of Lyle Hamel

(Figure 5.9). On another farm, north of the hill, the Graham family once received a handmade basket in exchange for a chicken. Skunk Hill people bought chickens, eggs, and even woodchucks from the Grimm family, who owned land adjacent to the hill.[21]

A grove of maple trees that regrew after the logging era also supplied one of the few natural resources available on the hill. Tapped in the spring, the sap was boiled to produce sugar maple syrup and sugar to be consumed, bartered, or sold. Figure 5.10 shows Cody Jackson, who owned ten acres of Skunk Hill land until 1926, at his sugar bush. In 2001, archaeologists from Archaeological Research Inc., working at the direction of the Wisconsin Historical Society, documented the remnant of a sugar maple boiling arch, perhaps Jackson's own, along with discarded cans used to collect the sap.[22] The remains had been discovered by James Scherz, formerly of the University of Wisconsin–Madison Department of Civil Engineering, during his own inspection of the hill. The arch is similar to those previously described for the McCord settlement.

Figure 5.10

Cody Jackson (left) with visitors at his maple sugar boiling operation at Skunk Hill | From the Carol Snowball Collection

The People

The permanent residents and many visitors of Skunk Hill are well documented in various historical sources and well-remembered by descendants and other area residents. A 1910 federal census for Arpin Township, where Skunk Hill is located, enumerates seventy-nine men, women, and children, most of whom are known to have lived at Skunk Hill or in its vicinity through other documents as well as oral history (see Appendix I). The census record is a "Special Inquiries Relating to Indians" that was taken in the early twentieth century along with the regular census.

The census lists twenty households, with some single male adults counted as separate households. Typical households consisted of a nuclear family, occasionally with a widowed and elderly parent of the husband or wife. The M-jig-no (Eagle Pigeon) and N-no-mo-qua household had three boarders, including Frank Link, later identified as an Ojibwe Drum Dance member who lived in a house in the lower community (Figure 5.11). In most cases, only Indian names were recorded, although generally the people also had Euro-American names and occasionally went by nicknames. Shortened versions of the Indian names were also used. For example, Sho-no-kuk-doos, also spelled Shoug-nuk-nok-uk, was commonly known as (John) Quatose, also spelled Kaudos.

As spelled in the 1910 census, the heads of households were as follows, with further identifications by the author in parentheses: Kich-kumme (Tom), Shogon-ne, Ed Wilson, Mazhis, Skum-ma, Wab-shawgain, Frank En-wash, M she kd, Pete Whitefish, Za-be-quak (Joe Cook), Mitchell, She-no-quik, Shea-no-yo-qua (likely Jim Spoon), Sho-no-kuk-doos (John Quatose or Kaudos), M-jig-no (Eagle Pigeon), John Nu-wee (John Nuwi/John Louis or Louis), Wa-Mas-Ka, Mem-Kwoot-Che, and Sham. Several other people are known to have lived there, such as Frank Young (who could be She-no-quick as listed in the census above) and family, close relatives of John Young and Cody Jackson, who later moved to McCord, as did Joe Cook and his wife and others.

The census identifies most of the people as Potawatomi, with most from Kansas and some born in Wisconsin. Other community

Figure 5.11

This labeled photograph from the collection of Carol Snowball includes Frank Link, Sam Link, George Anawash, Joe Waubanse, Peterson, and Charley Shegonne (*sic*), all in ceremonial regalia. The performance was probably the multitribal powwow, held August 11–14, 1921, in Wisconsin Rapids. The powwow was sponsored by the Wisconsin Rapids Chamber of Commerce and included Potawatomi, Ho-Chunk, Menominee, Ojibwe, Omaha from Nebraska, and the Sauk and Fox from Iowa. (See "Six Redskin Tribes Unite in Pow-Wow," *Milwaukee Journal*, June 5, 1921.) | From the Carol Snowball Collection

members were Ojibwe and Ho-Chunk, some of whom intermarried with the Potawatomi, along with one Kickapoo man from Kansas and one Potawatomi who was born in Mexico. (Some Potawatomi moved to Mexico along with a number of Kickapoo in the nineteenth century.[23])

Ten years later, in 1920, Skunk Hill had a slightly lower population of about seventy people, reflecting deaths in the community and movement of some to communities like McCord and elsewhere.[24] One tradition passed down among descendants is that of a "plague," or epidemic, that visited Skunk Hill. This may well be a remembrance of the catastrophic 1900–1901 smallpox outbreak that decimated John Young's Indian Farm village in Taylor County, which preceded Skunk Hill, but it may also refer to the lethal nationwide flu epidemic of 1917. The Wisconsin Winnebago Indian Agency at Grand Rapids (now Wisconsin Rapids) stated in its 1919 annual report that, lacking medical care, seventy-eight Indian people died during the influenza outbreak in the sixteen-county area of its jurisdiction in central and northern Wisconsin.[25] Another suspect is tuberculosis, a widespread killer in the early twentieth century.

The 1910 census data reveal that child mortality was high among the Indian people, as it was among settlers and the rural population as a whole at this time, and this may account for the large number of births recorded for some women. According to the census, twenty-eight-year-old M-Squash had given birth to eight children, two of whom had survived in 1910. Net-ge-gish-go-qua, age fifty-nine, had eight children, one living; Nom-kum-yo-quah, age forty-eight, had thirteen children, six living; and Koqua-wah, age forty-eight, had fourteen children with only three living. Most of the deaths would have occurred prior to residence at Skunk Hill.

Nevertheless, several people in the comparatively small community lived into their late eighties and nineties, which is remarkable considering that life expectancy for the general populace in 1920 was about fifty-four.[26] We might speculate that such longevity resulted from Big Drum dictates to live a virtuous life by staying away from alcohol and other vices, as well as the care and peace of mind that comes from a close family- and kinship-orientated community.

White Pigeon

Among the oldest of the Skunk Hill residents was White Pigeon, or Wab-me-me, whom many sources, including oral histories, identify as the informal leader of the community (Figure 5.12). White Pigeon came from the Kansas reservation in 1905; the 1910 census listed him as Potawatomi, but according to his descendants and other written sources he was a Ho-Chunk descended from those removed west in the early part of the nineteenth century. His death certificate says he was born in Iowa in 1840, and at that time the removed Ho-Chunk had been living in Iowa prior to removal to the Nebraska reservation.[27] He married a Prairie Band woman and lived on the Kansas reservation,

Figure 5.12

Alphonse Gerend identified the man on the left as White Pigeon. Rueben Young is the boy. | Alphonse Gerend Photo Album, Wisconsin Historical Society Archives; WHi Image ID 113824

where he became enrolled as a member of the Prairie Band Potawatomi, receiving a reservation allotment along with others.[28]

At least during the latter part of his life, White Pigeon lived in the lower community at Skunk Hill. Alphonse Gerend wrote that White Pigeon often recalled hunting buffalo on the Great Plains when he lived there on a western reservation and that he traveled between the Kansas reservation and Skunk Hill in his horse and buggy. White Pigeon remained at Skunk Hill until his death at age eighty-nine in 1931 and is buried there. Gerend identifies White Pigeon's son as Eagle Pigeon, also known as Eagle White Pigeon, who became a leader of the Drum Dance and also lived in the lower community.[29] There he owned forty acres with a fine barn and raised chickens, according to a neighboring farmer, Louis Grimm, who eventually bought his land.[30]

John Nuwi

While most residents came from the Prairie Band Potawatomi reservation on the Great Plains, others came from John Young's Taylor County Indian Farm community, including medicine man and keeper of the sacred Skunk Hill Drums John Nuwi, also known as John Louie or Louis, the most famous of the Skunk Hill residents (Figures 5.13a and 5.13b). Alanson Skinner featured Nuwi in his 1924 Milwaukee Public Museum publication *The Mascoutens or Prairie Potawatomi*. Like John Young and many others of the Wisconsin Prairie Band Potawatomi, John Nuwi's family came to southeastern Wisconsin from northeast Illinois.[31] Coincidentally, at one time he lived in a village located on the site where the Milwaukee Public Museum now stands, in the heart of the city.[32] Like other Wisconsin Prairie Potawatomi, he eventually moved to central Wisconsin to escape removal, living at various places along the route, and became an enrolled member of the Prairie Band Potowatomi reservation, receiving an allotment of land there under the Dawes Act of 1887. He never lived there but married a woman from the reservation who died sometime before Nuwi moved to Skunk Hill from the Indian Farms village in Taylor County. He was considered comparatively well off and was one of the original landowners of the Skunk Hill community.

Nuwi was considered a great orator and a widely known expert on Potawatomi history. He graciously shared his extensive traditional knowledge and personal stories with Skinner, Gerend, and others. Gerend, who met Nuwi in 1920, wrote that Nuwi lived alone in the woods in a new wood-frame house in the lower Skunk Hill community but preferred to live in a tent during the summer months.[33] Midwestern Native people traditionally lived in separate winter and summer dwellings. Nuwi hosted visitors from Kansas who came for ceremonies, and he sponsored feasts or "peace" dinners for them upon their departure at which he gave speeches.[34]

Figures 5.13a and 5.13b

Studio portrait (left) of John Nuwi, and Nuwi at his summer tent at Skunk Hill (right) | Both photos from the Alphonse Gerend Photograph Album, Wisconsin Historical Society Archives. (a) WHi Image ID 23946; (b) WHi Image ID 115095

Gerend also reported that Nuwi became the leader of the Skunk Hill community after White Pigeon, but Nuwi died in 1927, four years before White Pigeon. It is possible that Nuwi assumed informal leadership because White Pigeon was ailing, apparently losing his eyesight. Nuwi also died at an advanced age. He was buried in the cemetery on the hill that bears his name. One of his brothers is also reportedly interred at Skunk Hill.[35]

A Ceremonial Center

Ceremonial dances were held throughout the year at Skunk Hill and included a Sugar Dance in spring, a Harvest Dance in fall, the rites of the Midewiwin, and the major four-day Drum Dance.[36] The Drum Dance attracted Potawatomi, Ho-Chunk, and Ojibwe visitors from throughout the region as well as Prairie Band people from Kansas.

Visitors and participants came to the nearby town of Arpin by railroad or arrived at the hill by horse-drawn wagons, on horseback, or on foot. Automobiles undoubtedly were also used for transportation as they came into common use. One attendee was Chicog, a young man from the Lac du Flambeau Ojibwe Reservation who, like many Indian men, joined the US military and died during World War I (Figure 5.14a). Anna Goodvillage came from the nearby Ho-Chunk settlement of Hemlock Creek and "could be seen trudging along the country road leading her grandson by the hand and heavily burdened with bags and baskets as she slowly wound her way towards the hill"[37] (Figure 5.14b).

Figures 5.14a through 5.14e

Visitors to Skunk Hill included (a) Chicog; (b) Anna Goodvillage, seen here at her home at Hemlock Creek; (c) Kik-yak-o from Phlox; (d) Albert Thunder and family; and (e) John Mustache from McCord. | All images from Alphonse Gerend Photograph Album, Wisconsin Historical Society Archives: (a) WHi Image ID 113829; (b) WHi Image ID 113807; (c) WHi Image ID 113800; (d) WHi Image ID 113808; (e) WHi Image ID 113796

The elderly Kik-yak-o (Potawatomi/Ho-Chunk) lived in a Drum Dance community at Phlox near the Menominee Reservation but spent her summers at Skunk Hill visiting her daughter, Mrs. Spoon[38] (Figure 5.14c). Albert Thunder, a Ho-Chunk who had married a Potawatomi woman, also spent much time living at Skunk Hill and is pictured in Figure 5.14d with his family. Skunk Hill and McCord seemed to have rotated Drum Dance ceremonies, and some visitors to Skunk Hill came from McCord where some, like John Mustache, a respected leader, were key participants (Figure 5.14e). Since close relatives lived at both communities, individuals and families often spent periods of time living at both.

The main Drum Dance ceremony conducted at Skunk Hill followed the common pattern of the four-day rituals found elsewhere. A newspaper in nearby Vesper described an early Drum Dance ceremonial in October 1912 where "[o]n the summit of the hill the Indians have scalped of an arena about sixty or seventy feet in diameter. The sods taken off were piled up to a suitable place to sit down, and the arena was enclosed with a fence. At the entrance of the arena three American flags were hoisted and one large white flag."[39]

In this ceremonial, four Drums suspended by staffs and decorated with beads, feathers, and other objects were used during subsequent days of singing, dancing, and feasting. Offerings of tobacco and ritual smoking of tobacco in stone pipes with long wooden stems were important parts of the ceremonies. The newspaper account does not describe the rituals and dances in much detail and quotes White Pigeon saying, "The Indians do not like to have white people around when they dance. Much less would they allow anybody to take pictures."[40]

In 1923, however, Alphonse Gerend attended a similar four-day ceremonial and noted that non-Indian spectators at that time were welcome at the ceremonies but could not take pictures until the last afternoon.[41] It is probable that over the years Skunk Hill residents became more comfortable with spectators, who were now considered neighbors and friends, and grew proud of showing their way of life that promoted peace, brotherhood, and virtue.

Gerend wrote that the 1923 ceremonials were conducted in the Potawatomi language and that Eagle Pigeon, the eldest son of White Pigeon, was a leader. The Link brothers, William and James, served as masters of ceremony, and the elders White Pigeon, Jim Young, John Nuwi, and John Mustache gave speeches (Figure 5.15). During the ceremonies, drummers moved to each of the four drums. A group of women accompanied the drumming with chants and singing. Many participants wore full ceremonial regalia and had their faces painted with red stripes and other markings. Over the course of the four days, feasts were held and gifts were distributed to participants. On the fourth day, Gerend reported, an eagle feather war bustle played a special role.[42]

Figure 5.15

William Link, master of ceremonies at the
1923 ceremonials | Alphonse Gerend Photograph
Album, Wisconsin Historical Society Archives; WHi Image
ID 113826

Other important and much older ceremonials conducted at Skunk
Hill were the rites of the Grand Medicine Society, or Midewiwin, conducted in a very long, open-walled medicine lodge constructed with
posts bent over at the top in the style of a wigwam (Figure 5.16). The
Midewiwin is a curing and healing society, still active today, that has
its roots in antiquity and is found throughout the upper midwestern
and Great Lakes tribes, including the Potawatomi, Ojibwe, Ottawa, and

Figure 5.16

A medicine lodge, partly covered by canvas, and unidentified person at Skunk Hill. The fence surrounding a dance circle can be seen through the trees on the right. | Alphonse Gerend Photograph Album, Wisconsin Historical Society Archives; WHi Image ID 113830

Ho-Chunk. The society consists of Native doctors and priests, who undergo many years of training in holistic medicine, attending to patients through rituals and with medicines made from special plants. Practitioners come together periodically to induct new members. As a medicine man, John Nuwi almost certainly was as active in these ceremonies at Skunk Hill as he was in the Drum Dance.

The Demise of Skunk Hill

From about seventy people in 1920, the population of Skunk Hill greatly dwindled through the next decade. By 1928, the upper village on top of the hill had been mostly abandoned and the land sold to non-Indian landowners. In that year, fifteen people lived on the hill, according to a letter from Potawatomi Daniel Shepard of Carter, Wisconsin, to Charles E. Brown at the Wisconsin Historical Society. Most had been living at Skunk Hill in 1910. These were (as spelled in the document): John Quatose (Shoug-nuck-ku-uck); Mrs. Quatose and her brother; Charles Shogonne (Kaw-ka-you-ko-uck) and Mille Shog-onee; White Pigeon; Eagle Pigeon (M-zhuckno) and wife Ano-mo-quah; Russell Barnes (B-kish-shin); James Pigeon and Mrs. Rebecca Pigeon; Mrs. Kitchkumme (Nu-kom-go-quah) and son Thomas Kitchcumme (Pot-ku-shuck); Winnebago (Ho-Chunk) Frank Winne-shick; and Menominee Mrs. Jane Winneshick. Shepard wrote that the Frank Young family had recently moved from Skunk Hill.[43] A few Potawatomi people remained at the base of the hill for many years just south of where Powers Bluff County Park was established in the 1930s. Ahn-mo-quah (same as Ano-moquah above) and her son by a first marriage, Russell Barnes, are listed in 1948 as owning contiguous parcels of land, twenty acres each, identified as "Indian Land" in the Wood County plat book for that year.[44]

The demise of the ceremonial community was gradual as the founders died and other residents moved away to make better livings. Some moved east, closer to the city of Wisconsin Rapids, while others headed west to a place called Poppleland. Still others moved to the McCord ceremonial community, which offered more resources from which to obtain a living. As the population dwindled, the Drum Dance ceremonials also shifted to McCord, according to the elders.[45]

Certainly the Great Depression itself would have affected the residents of Skunk Hill as it did everyone to one extent or another, and some of the Indian-owned land reportedly was lost because of nonpayment of local property taxes. The oral history says that several women were forced to leave the lands, moving to the Kansas reservation.[46] Deeds are not clear on the matter. In another cases it is unclear how Indian-owned property was transferred to non-Indian people because deeds do not record the transactions.[47]

But some of the Indian landowners had already begun to sell their land in the latter part of the 1920s. Cody Jackson sold his ten acres in 1926 and was known to be living at McCord. John Nuwi's land, also ten acres, was sold in the year of his death in 1927 for $125.[48] As mentioned earlier, Eagle Pigeon eventually sold his land to a neighboring farmer.

With the Meriam Report of 1928 and the Indian Reorganization Act of 1934, the forced assimilation period—the Great Suppression—was also at an end. These acts greatly lessened the need for special off-reservation communities among those who sought to maintain traditional ways. The disastrous allotment policy was terminated, and what was left of Indian land returned to tribal ownership. Nevertheless, many of Skunk Hill's descendants continue to live not far from the original village (Figure 5.17). Today they form a modern community that is rooted in traditional Potawatomi culture and where the Big Drum, as it is now called, continues to provide guidance. In most other places, the Drum Dance ceremonial faded in importance for a long time, making a resurgence only in recent years.[49] But among the descendants of Skunk Hill, the Drum Dance way of life has been passed down continuously through the generations. For them and many others, Skunk Hill is an inspiration and a powerful symbol of cultural persistence—a place where the cultural fire was kept burning, as appropriate for the role of the Potawatomi as "Keepers of Fire" in the Indian world during a time when outside forces tried to extinguish it.

Figure 5.17

Many of the descendants of Skunk Hill people gathered at Skunk Hill in 2000. | Photo courtesy of Art and Dawn Shegonne

6

Skunk Hill in History and Today

AFTER THE INDIAN PEOPLE moved away and the land passed to others, the old village at Powers Bluff was briefly used for cattle grazing. Only one deserted cabin remained near the top of the hill in 1933. In that same year, the Wood County township of Arpin picked up fifty acres on the hill for back taxes from the estate of H. F. Roehring and land sold by his survivor. The township in turn conveyed the land to Wood County to establish a large and scenic park.[1] Workers employed by the Depression-era Civil Works Administration and the Wisconsin Emergency Relief Administration cleared the woods and built park roads with the assistance of area farmers working off government loans. A new county road was extended along the south boundary of the new park, providing public access. Workers constructed a log park shelter at the top of the hill, near where log cabins once stood, and enclosed the two cemeteries with rock walls. The two Drum Dance rings were also preserved during park development and remain today next to the parking area at the top of the hill.

Wood County acquired more land for Powers Bluff Park through the years, developing the steep north slope opposite the historic village into a winter recreation area that offers skiing, sledding, and most recently tubing. In 1976 the Wisconsin Department of Natural Resources designated seventy acres of the eastern part of the park as Maple Woods Natural Area, owing to the beautiful forest and rare plants growing there.

When Wood County made its plan to cut trees that covered the former Skunk Hill village in order to thin and manage the forest in 2000, conflict arose over the public use of the park. Some residents protested, stating that tree thinning would disrupt the ecology of the area, which included the seasonal blooms of brightly colored flowers. Descendants of the Skunk Hill community as well other Native people brought forth concerns about the effect of the tree cutting on important plants used for medicines, and about the general impact of increased recreational use of the park, including plans to expand the ski and tubing hill on the north slope. The concerns drew the attention of the western Prairie Band Potawatomi Nation government since the local Potawatomi are enrolled members of the reservation, and the Ho-Chunk Nation. Meetings and discussions, some of them contentious, were held among the concerned parties. Skunk Hill once again made local and state news, adding to the tensions.[2] The Division of Historic Preservation at the Wisconsin Historical Society became involved because of its responsibility to protect all burial sites and cemeteries under the state's burial protection law, Section 157.70 of Wisconsin Statutes. But soon concerns extended to protection of the entire old community as a historic place. Unfortunately, descriptions and other information about the Skunk Hill community had never been compiled, and even the extent of the Skunk Hill community was uncertain.

After the controversy began, my office at the time—that of state archaeologist at the Wisconsin Historical Society—offered to conduct objective research to determine the boundaries and contents of the area that once constituted the Skunk Hill community and thereby establish the areas of Powers Bluff County Park that needed protection. (The state archaeologist has the general responsibility of identifying and protecting the state's archaeological sites, particularly those on public lands.) Our goal was to produce a nomination for the National Register of Historic Places, working with the Wood County Park and Forestry Department, Native people, and others to gather information concerning the Skunk Hill community. A property listed on the National Register of Historic Places can be protected if proposed development projects use federal money or involve a federal agency, such as those requiring federal permits. Sites on the National Register are also listed on the State Register of Historic Places maintained by the Wisconsin Historical Society. When located on state- or local-government-owned land, places designated to these registers also receive some protections under Wisconsin law. In the case of political subdivisions, such as counties, officials are required under Section 66.111 of Wisconsin Statutes to at least consult on proposed actions that might disturb the historic place. In all cases, the advantages of a listing on the national and state registers for landowners and the public are that specific areas deserving protection are defined and explanations are given as to why the properties are important to national, state, or local history. National and state register status also helps draw public attention and appreciation to the place. However, all burial places are protected by state laws (Section 170.70 Wisconsin Statues) that prevent the disturbance of graves without a thorough review, which includes consultation with interested parties, such as living relatives and other tribal representatives.

The 2000 study incorporated the rich historical and pictorial records pertaining to Skunk Hill; oral history obtained from elders who lived on the hill as children, from descendants of the community, and from other older people who lived near the community; and a physical examination of the park in the form of archaeological surveys. The controversy reached the halls of the state capitol, and in response the state legislature approved a small allocation to the Wisconsin Historical Society to fund the study and help resolve the matter.

The archaeological research, coordinated by the Office of the State Archaeologist, brought together a team of experts who in 2000–2001 employed a number of techniques to locate the physical remains of the village. These included visual inspections of the land; using nondisturbing ground-penetrating remote-sensing equipment in the area of the documented village on the top of the south slope; and the excavation of hundreds of small holes with shovels (called shovel probes) at close intervals in the wooded and undisturbed areas within the winter recreation lands on the north slope. The shovel probes were accompanied by the use of a metal detector to locate artifacts and old disturbances that would identify potential areas of activity associated with the Skunk Hill community.[3]

The research documented many features—such as vestiges of structures and the sugar bush that had been mostly covered by earth and vegetation, and a segment of a trail used by people long before modern roads were built—that attested to the existence of a once vital community on the south side of the bluff, beyond the burial grounds and dance rings. The surveys were assisted by that fateful storm in the summer of 2001 that toppled many trees at the eastern edge of the documented community, exposing a several-acre field of debris from the late nineteenth or early twentieth century that had the potential to add much information to the known history of the hill. The debris included broken dishware, and pieces of lanterns, stoves, and metal containers that might be from the village or from John Arpin's earlier logging camp. During the study, the Wisconsin Historical Society formally cataloged the two cemeteries as burial places, and they are thus protected under Wisconsin's burial site protection law. It is possible that other graves exist outside the cemeteries; however, no evidence was found indicating that the Skunk Hill community extended down the north slope below the prominent rock outcrops where the Powers Bluff winter recreation area is located. This is logical, since the base of the slope is moist and marshy, and locating part of the settlement there would have exposed it to cold winter winds.

On April 12, 2002, Potawatomi and Ho-Chunk people from central Wisconsin went to the Wisconsin Historical Society in Madison to honor Skunk Hill by witnessing and supporting an important event. On that day, the fifteen-member Historic Preservation Review Board held its quarterly meeting to consider nominations to the National Register of Historic Places for the state of Wisconsin. Among the nominations to be considered that day was that of Tah-qua-kik, or Skunk Hill, compiled from the extensive research conducted between 2000 and 2002.

The Native people were joined in the boardroom by representatives of the Prairie Band Potawatomi Nation, whose people once formed the nucleus of the Skunk Hill community. The Prairie Band Potawatomi also sent a tribal council resolution endorsing the nomination, and a representative of the Wood County Board attended to show support. About seventy-five people crowded the small room, the largest number of people to attend a public meeting of the Historic Preservation Review Board up to that time. After hearing the presentation and testimonies by many, the review board approved the nomination to loud applause and cheers.[4]

The Skunk Hill nomination was subsequently reviewed and approved by the National Register of Historic Places and listed on the registry in 2003, joining the two related ceremonial communities founded by Drum Dance leader John Young at Indian Farms in Taylor County (listed in 1988) and McCord in Oneida County (listed in 2001). Today, eighty acres in the south half of Powers Bluff County Park are designated as a protected area on the National Registry.

In historical terms, the remnants of Skunk Hill and the other Drum Dance ceremonial communities are significant because of their unique histories as places where Native traditions, values, and ceremonies were maintained during a period of harsh US government policies to forcefully assimilate Native people into the broader and dominant American culture. The preserved elements of the communities, such as the dance rings, highlight this importance.

For Native people, however, the significance of Skunk Hill goes far beyond its historical value. It is a sacred place. "Skunk Hill means a place where my ancestors visited, lived, and died," stated Prairie Band Potawatomi tribal council member Rey Kitchkumme in 2001. "It's a part of my history and culture. It's similar to what would be called a church where people congregate and connect with the spiritual life."[5]

Wood County subsequently completed a master plan for Powers Bluff County Park with public input, both Native and non-Native, in order to accommodate recreational use of the park while preserving the remnants of the Skunk Hill community.[6] Based on information provided in the National Register nomination, the acres set aside on the south slope of Powers Bluff have been designated as an historic or cultural area to be carefully protected and managed. The plan also recommended acquisition of 223 acres north of the park so that winter recreation facilities and parking can be moved from the top of the hill, where they share space with part of the historic Skunk Hill community, to a location at the north base of Powers Bluff. The acquisition was made in 2012.

In the meantime, Skunk Hill continues to be a gathering place for descendants of the original community members. And the story of Skunk Hill provides an important reminder and lesson for us all about a time not that long ago when the principle of religious freedom upon which this nation was founded was withheld from many residing within its borders, a time when the practice of certain cultural traditions and religious beliefs was oppressed by the US government with the assent of much of the American public in an effort to create, in essence, one homogeneous Christian nation, eliminating indigenous cultures and their worldviews in the process.

Appendix I:

Data for Skunk Hill and Vicinity from the
Thirteenth Census of the United States, 1910,
Special Inquiries Relating to Indians,
Arpin Township, Wood County, Wisconsin,
with Additional Notes by the Author

Note: Names are spelled as they appear on the census, and appear by household with the head of household listed in bold.

Name	Sex	Age	Tribe	Annotations CD: Census Data; AN: Author Notes	Birthplace
Kich-cumme (head)	M	50	Potawatomi	CD: Second marriage. AN: Also spelled Kitchkumme. First name Tom. Held an allotment on the Prairie Band Potawatomi (PBP) Reservation (Appendix 2). Interred at Skunk Hill.	Kansas
Nom-kum-quah (wife)	F	48	Potawatomi	CD: 13 children, 6 living. AN: Daughter of Drum Dance leader John Young.	Kansas
Nellie (daughter)	F	25	Potawatomi	CD: Widowed	Kansas
Tommie (son)	M	13	Potawatomi		Kansas
Shogon-ne (head)	M	47	Potawatomi	AN: Held an allotment on the PBP Reservation (Appendix 2).	Kansas
Koqua-wah (wife)	F	48	Potawatomi	CD: 14 children, 3 living	Wisconsin
Koa-ka-yo-ank (son)	M	12	Potawatomi		Kansas
Sn-na-kate (son)	M	9	Potawatomi		Kansas
Ah-no-bwa-she (son)	M	3	Potawatomi		Wisconsin
Ed Wilson (head)	M	21	Winnebago	CD: Received an allotment on the PBP Reservation in 1902.	Wisconsin
Ethel (wife)	F	18	Potawatomi		Kansas

Name	Sex	Age	Tribe	Annotations CD: Census Data; AN: Author Notes	Birthplace
Rot-ko	M	70	Potawatomi		Kansas
Maghis (head)	M	26	Potawatomi	CD: Received an allotment on the PBP Reservation in 1904.	Kansas
N-skuck-kah-quah (wife)	F	26	Potawatomi	CD: 6 children, 3 living	Wisconsin
Minnie (daughter)	F	5	Potawatomi		Kansas
Carrie (daughter)	F	2	Potawatomi		Kansas
Johnson (son)	M	1 mo.	Potawatomi		Wisconsin
Skum-ma (head)	M	24	Potawatomi	AN: Likely the Schum-nah who held an allotment on the PBP Reservation.	Kansas
Annie (wife)	F	20	Potawatomi		Wisconsin
Son not yet named	M	1 mo.	Potawatomi		Kansas
Wab-shawgain (head)	M	64	Potawatomi	CD: Second marriage. AN: Likely the Wab-shog-gin who held an allotment on the PBP Reservation (Appendix 2).	Kansas
Ke-we-she (wife)	F	26	Potawatomi	CD: Second marriage; 5 children, 2 living	Kansas
John (son)	M	4	Potawatomi		Wisconsin
Frank En-wash (head)	M	28	Chippewa		Wisconsin
Ob-weg (wife)	F	26	Potawatomi		Kansas
John (son)	M	7	Chippewa/ Potawatomi		Wisconsin
George (son)	M	5	Chippewa/ Potawatomi		Kansas
Net-ge-gish-go-qwa (mother)	F	59	Chippewa	CD: Widowed mother of Frank; 8 children, 1 living	Wisconsin
M she kd (head)	M	30	Potawatomi	AN: Likely M-she-kah who held an allotment on the PBP Reservation (Appendix 2).	Wisconsin
M-Squash (wife)	F	28	Chippewa	CD: 8 children, 2 living	Wisconsin
Now-qwa-quish-k-qua (daughter)	F	7	Potawatomi		Wisconsin

Name	Sex	Age	Tribe	Annotations CD: Census Data; AN: Author Notes	Birthplace
Charlie (son)	M	5	Chippewa/ Potawatomi		Wisconsin
Pete Whitefish (head)	M	37	Chippewa		Wisconsin
Gub-Wes-Ma (wife)	F	41	Potawatomi	CD: 2 children, 1 living	Wisconsin
Sh?-watum-mo-gui (daughter)	F	2	Chippewa/ Potawatomi		Wisconsin
Za-be-quak (head)	M	33	Potawatomi	CD: Second marriage. AN: Also known as Joe Cook, whose Indian name was also listed as Kah-so-be-tuck in allotment records (Appendix 2).	Wisconsin
Ke-o-kum-ma-qua (wife)	F	30	Potawatomi	CD: 3 children. AN: Held an allotment on the PBP Reservation (Appendix 2). She was co-owner of land at Skunk Hill with her mother, Mik-sik-qua, below.	Kansas
N-te-quish (son)	M	9	Potawatomi	CD: Received an allotment at the PBP Reservation in 1903	Kansas
Pem-ma-tik	M	7	Potawatomi	CD: Received an allotment at the PBP Reservation in 1903	Kansas
In-sway-ash (son)	M	2	Potawatomi		Wisconsin
Mik-sik-qua (mother-in-law)	F	65	Potawatomi	CD: Widowed mother of Ke-o-kum-ma-qua. AN: Also spelled Mixequa/Mexico/ Mix-such-quah. Co-owner of land at Skunk Hill. Likely the Meeksaquish interred at Skunk Hill, she held an allotment on the PBP Reservation (Appendix 2).	Kansas
Mitchell (head)	M	50	Potawatomi		Wisconsin

Name	Sex	Age	Tribe	Annotations CD: Census Data; AN: Author Notes	Birthplace
She-no-quik (head)	M	45	Potawatomi	CD: Second marriage. AN: Possibly Frank Young, known to have owned land at Skunk Hill. Early ownership records for 1914 also give the name Shu-wa-quock, while later records include Frank Young.	Kansas
Quit-a-ko-qua (wife)	F	50	Chippewa	CD: Second marriage	Wisconsin
Mek-gui-osh (son)	M	12	Chippewa/ Potawatomi		Wisconsin
Sag-jo-a-qwa (son)	M	5	Chippewa/ Potawatomi		Wisconsin
Knw-ta-see (son)	M	2	Chippewa/ Potawatomi		Wisconsin
Shea-na-yo-qua (head)	M	48	Potawatomi	CD: Widowed; 3 children. AN: Possible original owner of land at Skunk Hill and likely the individual known as Jim Spoon.	Wisconsin
Ket-gon-guit (son)	M	27	Potawatomi		Wisconsin
Nish-ke-we-teck (son)	M	22	Potawatomi		Wisconsin
Pe-moo-nook (daughter)	F	14	Potawatomi		Wisconsin
Kno-quish-ka (father)	M	70	Potawatomi	CD: Widowed father of Shea-na-yo-qua. AN: Likely Wab-kesh-go (Bill Spoon) who died in 1914 and is interred at Skunk Hill.	Wisconsin
White Pigeon (head)	M	64	Potawatomi /Ho-Chunk	AN: Was actually Ho-Chunk but enrolled as member of the PBP Reservation and held an allotment there. Owned land on Skunk Hill and is interred there.	Kansas
Rosie (wife)	F	50	Potawatomi		Wisconsin

Name	Sex	Age	Tribe	Annotations CD: Census Data; AN: Author Notes	Birthplace
Wubo-kon-kate (daugher)	F	15	Potawatomi		Kansas
Wah-on-i-qot-che-qua (son)	M	21	Potawatomi	AN: Likely Wah-on-i-zib-che-qua, who held an allotment on the PBP Reservation (Appendix 2).	Iowa
Sha-o-no-en (mother-in-law)	F	80	Potawatomi /Winnebago	CD: Widowed mother of Rosie	Illinois
Sho-no-kuk-doos (head)	M		Potawatomi	AN: Also known as John Quatose or Kaudos. Held an allotment on the PBP Reservation (Appendix 2). Owner of land at Skunk Hill. Interred at Skunk Hill.	Kansas
Sa-niw-ne-quah (wife)	F	34	Potawatomi	CD: 5 children. AN: Mary Quatose or Kaudos	Iowa
Kay-a-kum (daughter)	F	9	Potawatomi		Kansas
Shan-n-vin (daughter)	F	8	Potawatomi		Kansas
Wesh-k-sha (daughter	F	6	Potawatomi		Kansas
Gish-go-qua (daughter)	F	2	Potawatomi		Wisconsin
Ka-pas-sa (son)	M	2 mo.	Potawatomi		Wisconsin
M-jig-no (head)	M	36	Potawatomi /Winnebago	AN: The oldest son of White Pigeon, also known as Eagle Pigeon and M-Shunk-No, he also owned land at Skunk Hill. M-Shunk-no held an allotment number that immediately followed that of White Pigeon (Appendix 2).	Iowa
N-no-mo-qua (wife)	F	50	Potawatomi	CD: Second marriage; 3 children, 1 living. Later owned land at Skunk Hill in her name.	Kansas

Name	Sex	Age	Tribe	Annotations CD: Census Data; AN: Author Notes	Birthplace
Russel Barnes (stepson)	M	6	Potawatomi /white	AN: Owned land at Skunk Hill as an adult next to his mother, N-no-mo-qua, above.	Kansas
Puak-mash-ke-tap-see (boarder)	M	21	Potawatomi		Wisconsin
Ob-tee koo (boarder)	M	9	Potawatomi		Kansas
Frank Link (boarder)	M	25	Chippewa	CD: Widowed	Wisconsin
John Nu-wee (head)	M	60	Potawatomi	AN: Also spelled Nuwi, and also known as John Louie/Louis. Medicine man and owner of land at Skunk Hill. Nu-wee held an allotment on the PBP Reservation (Appendix 2). He died in 1927 and is interred at Skunk Hill.	Wisconsin
Kaw-ta-gish-kuk (wife)	F	60	Potawatomi	CD: 8 children, 1 living. AN: She died before John and is likely interred at Skunk Hill.	Kansas
Wa-Mas-Ka (head)	M	30	Potawatomi	CD: Second marriage. AN: Possibly the Wah-was-sah who held an allotment on the PBP Reservation (Appendix 2).	Mexico
Ruth (wife)	F	24	Potawatomi		Kansas
Wab-ke-shik (son)	M	2	Potawatomi		Kansas
Wem-Kwoot-Che (head)	M		Kickapoo	CD: Widowed	Kansas
Sham (head)	M	40	Potawatomi	CD: Widowed. AN: Also spelled Shohm. Co-owner of land at Skunk Hill in 1914. Possibly the Schum-nah who sold an allotment on the PBP Reservation.	Wisconsin

Name	Sex	Age	Tribe	Annotations CD: Census Data; AN: Author Notes	Birthplace
Sueg-quish-kink-qua (daughter)	F	16	Potawatomi	AN: Also spelled Squagishgoquah on Skunk Hill property ownership documents. Co-owner of land with her father, Sham, at Skunk Hill in 1914. Possibly the Squash-gish-go-quah who held an allotment on the PBP Reservation (Appendix 2).	Wisconsin
Me-o-was-ke (son)	M	13	Potawatomi		Wisconsin

Appendix 2:

Roll of Prairie Potawatomi with Reservation Allotments Living in Wisconsin circa 1918, with Notes by the Author*

Note: Names are spelled as they appear on the allotment documents. Individuals believed to have lived at Skunk Hill are in bold.

Name	Allotment No.	Author's Notes
An-a-wa	736	
Angeline (Cook)	203	Possibly the wife of Joe Cook who lived at Skunk Hill and McCord, but also see entries for Keo-ko-mo-quah below.
Ash-to-kish-ko-quah	82	
Ash-puck (Shock-to)	302	
Ash-to-yosh-no-quar	752	
Da-bash	718	
Dwa-ah-be	772	
Kack-kack	731	
Kah-kin-kote	56	Most likely Cody Jackson (also spelled Kat-kin-kate), who lived at Skunk Hill and McCord.
Kah-so-be-tuck (Joe Cook)	257	Most likely Za-be-quak from the 1910 Arpin Township Indian census (Appendix 1). Joe Cook is known to have lived at Skunk Hill and McCord.
Kaw-kah-you-ko-uck	738	
Kaw-to-gish-co-quah	749	Probably Kaw-ta-gish-kuk, wife of John Nuwi of Skunk Hill, Nu-wee on the 1910 Arpin Township Indian census (Appendix 1).
Ke-was-sah	798	Possibly Ke-we-she, wife of Wab-shawgain on the 1910 Arpin Township Indian census (Appendix 1).

*William Elsey Connelley, ed. "The Prairie Band of Pottawatomie Indians," in *Collections of the Kansas State Historical Society, 1915–1918,* Vol. XIV, 1918, 555–570.

Name	Allotment No.	Author's Notes
Ke-ah-we (Annie LeClare)	107	
Keo-ko-mo-quah, Wam-ta-ko-she	606	Possibly Ke-o-kum-ma-qua, wife of Za-be-quak (believed to be Joe Cook), and daughter of Mik-sik-qua in the 1910 Arpin Township Indian census (Appendix 1) .
Keo-o-ko-mo-quah (Jas. Wauhb-no-sah)	607	
Ke-note-ko	286	
Kish-kote	730	
Kitch-kum-me, Thomas	673	Most likely Tom Kich-cumme of Skunk Hill in the 1910 Arpin Township Indian census (Appendix 1).
Kitch-kum-me, Julia Ann	311	
Kow-to-gish-ko-quah	51	
Ko-ko-mo-quah	95	
Ko-mo-no-quah	708	
Kotch-ka-yotch-wen	778	
Mac-tah-kone-yah-quah	794	
Mat-twoash-she	714	
M-daw-che	360	
M-daw-che, Rebecca (Shock-to)	612	
M-daw-che, John (Shock-to)	610	
Meaugh-was-kah	525	Possibly Me-o-was-ke, son of Sham on the 1910 Arpin Township Indian census (Appendix 1).
M-ko-meese	806	
M-nis-no-quah, M-nis-no-quoh	729	
Mis-co-tah-quah	783	
M-she-kah	671	Most likely M she kd on the 1910 Arpin Township Indian census (Appendix 1) .

Name	Allotment No.	Author's Notes
M-shunk-no	438	Most likely M-jig-no on the1910 Arpin Township Indian census (Appendix 1), also known as Eagle Pigeon, eldest son of White Pigeon. His allotment number also follows that of Eagle Pigeon (437).
M-she-kah	211	Possibly N-te-quish, oldest son of Za-be-quak in the 1910 Arpin Township Indian census (Appendix 1).
M-suck-no	43	
Mix-such-quah	132	Likely Mik-se-quah, mother of Ke-o-kum-ma-qua in the 1910 Arpin Township Indian census (Appendix 1).
N-wee	546	John Nuwi of Skunk Hill, also known as John Louie or Louis.
Nah-bah-kah	758	
O-ge-mah-quah	793	
O-muck-ko	803	
Op-te-gish-ko-quah	92	
Po-way	789	
Pam-wa-tuck	782	
Pa-se-quck	757	
Pen-na-sa-quick	771	Possibly Pem-ma-tik, second son of Za-be-quak in the 1910 Arpin Township Indian census (Appendix 1).
Pe-qua-no, Alfred	551	
P-yet-ta-sen	759	
Quin-nah-kah	744	
Schum-nah (land sold)	435	Possibly Skum-ma or Sham, both in the 1910 Arpin Township Indian census (Appendix 1).
She-kone-nee	734	Likely Shogon-ne of Skunk Hill in the 1910 Arpin Township Indian census.
Shough-non-kote	739	
Shug-naab-go-quah	560	Possibly Shea-no-yo-qua in the 1910 Arpin Township Indian census (Appendix 1).

Name	Allotment No.	Author's Notes
Sheppos, James	691	
Sheppo, Frank (land sold)	38	
Shebah-kah-gak (dead)	295	
Shough-nab-no-noquot	706	
Shough-nuk-ko-uck, Jane	377	
Shough-nuk-ko-uk (Quotose)	375	John Quatose, who lived at Skunk Hill and is listed as Sho-no-kuk-doos in the 1910 Arpin Township Indian census (Appendix 1).
Sow-now-no-quah	376	Appears as Sa-niw-ne-quah, wife of John Quatose, on the 1910 Arpin Township Indian census (Appendix 1). Also called Mary. Her allotment number follows that of John Quatose (375).
Shough-nuk-uk (John Young)	547	Possibly the Wisconsin Drum Dance leader John Young, also known as Nsowakwet.
Squa-ge-shick	760	
Squash-gish-go-quah	524	Possibly Sueg-quish-kink-qua, daughter of Sham, in the 1910 Arpin Township Indian census (Appendix 1).
Ta-bash-sa-quah	719	
Te-cum-seh	732	
T-pis-sum	781	
Wab-shog-gin	434	Likely Wab-shawgain in the 1910 Arpin Township Indian census (Appendix 1) .
Wahb-walk	433	
Wab-shon-quit-to-quah	704	
Wab-shuck-ko-uk (dead, land sold)	537	
Wah-walk-sum	796	
Wah-saah-kuck	536	
Wah-was-sah	745	Possibly Wa-Mas-Ka in the 1910 Arpin Township Indian census (Appendix 1) .
Wah-tos-ka	784	

Name	Allotment No.	Author's Notes
Wah-on-i-zib-che-qua	441	Possibly Wah-on-i-qot-che-qua, who is listed as a son of White Pigeon of Skunk Hill in the 1910 Arpin Township Indian census (Appendix 1).
Wap-kesh-go	430	Likely Kno-quish-ka (Bill Spoon) in the 1910 Arpin Township Indian census (Appendix 1). Also spelled Wau-kesh-go.
Was-cho-wen-no-quah	751	
Waub-me-me (Iowa)	437	White Pigeon of Skunk Hill, born in Iowa.
Way-we-yah-kesh-kote	766	
Zow-kish-ko-quah	715	
Zo-ko-ke-shuck, land sold	535	

Notes

NOTES TO CHAPTER 1:

1. Thomas Vennum, *The Ojibwe Dance Drum: Its History and Construction*, Rev. ed. (Minneapolis: Minnesota Historical Society Press, 2009).

2. Harold Hickerson, "The Southwestern Chippewa: An Ethno-Historical Study," *American Anthropological Association* 64, no. 3, part 2 (1962), 69–70.

3. George T. Amour, "A Personal Account: My Birthplace, McCord Indian Village." McCord site file, Office of the State Archaeologist, Wisconsin Historical Society, Madison, WI.

4. Nancy Oestrich Lurie, *Wisconsin Indians: Revised and Expanded Edition* (Madison: Wisconsin Historical Society Press, 2002), 36–37.

5. Gary Mitchell, "Tribal History," Prairie Band Potawatomi website, www.pbpindiantribe.com/tribal-history.aspx.

6. Lurie, *Wisconsin Indians*, 36–37.

7. Douglas Collins, *The Story of Kodak* (New York: Henry N. Abrams, 1990).

8. Among these was Wisconsin's H. H. Bennett, who marketed studio and outdoor pictures of Ho-Chunk people in Wisconsin Dells for tourists. See Steven D. Hoelscher, *Picturing Indians* (Madison: University of Wisconsin Press, 2008). Some Native people also had pictures taken of themselves as keepsakes and as gifts for friends and family members; see Tom Jones, "A Ho-Chunk Photographer Looks at Charles Van Schaick," in Tom Jones, Michael Schmudlach, Matthew Daniel Mason, Amy Lonetree, and George A. Greendeer, *People of the Big Voice: Photographs of Ho-Chunk Families by Charles Van Schaick, 1879–1942* (Madison: Wisconsin Historical Society Press, 2011), 25.

9. See, for example, a lengthy article written by Gerend for the May 28, 1932, issue of *The Sheboygan Press* titled "Traditions and Customs of the Once Powerful Indian Tribes That Roamed over the State of Wisconsin."

10. Letter, Daniel Shepard to Charles E. Brown, June 28, 1928, Charles E. Brown Papers, Box 48, Wood County file, Wisconsin Historical Society Archives, Madison, WI.

11. Brookings Institution, *The Problem of Indian Administration: Report of a Survey made at the request of Honorable Hubert Work, Secretary of the Interior, and submitted to him, February 21, 1928, Baltimore, Md.* (Baltimore: The Johns Hopkins Press, 1928), 3.

12. Lurie, *Wisconsin Indians*, 40–41.

NOTES TO CHAPTER 2:

1. For an overview of American Indian policies from 1776 to present, see Nancy Bonvillain, *Native Nations of North America* (New York: Pearson, 2001), 17–35.

2. Mark Hirsh, "Thomas Jefferson: Founding Father of Indian Removal," *National Museum of the American Indian* 11, no. 2 (2009): 54–58.

3. Gloria Jahoda, *Trail of Tears: The Story of the American Indian Removal, 1813–1855* (New York: Henry Holt, 1995).

4. James A. Clifton, "Wisconsin Death March: Explaining the Extremes in Old Northwest Indian Removal," *Transactions of the Wisconsin Academy of Sciences, Arts and Letters* 75 (1987): 1–40; Patty Loew, *Indian Nations of Wisconsin: Histories of Endurance and Renewal*, 2nd ed. (Madison: Wisconsin Historical Society Press, 2013), 66–69.

5. Loew, *Indian Nations of Wisconsin*, 128.

6. Nancy Oestrich Lurie, *Wisconsin Indians: Revised and Expanded Edition* (Madison: Wisconsin Historical Society Press, 2002), 36.

7. Ibid., 37.

8. Ibid., 39.

9. Ibid., 37.

10. For a summary of these with respect to Wisconsin Indian Native Nations, see Loew, *Indian Nations of Wisconsin*, and Lurie, *Wisconsin Indians*.

11. David Edmunds, *The Potawatomi: Keepers of the Fire* (Norman: University of Oklahoma Press, 1987), 33–34.

12. James A. Clifton, "Potawatomi," in *Handbook of North America Indians*, vol. 15, ed. Bruce G. Trigger (Washington, DC: Smithsonian Institution, 1978), 732–733; Robert F. Sasso and Dan Joyce, "Ethnohistory and Archaeology: The Removal Era Potawatomi Lifeway in Southwestern Wisconsin," *MidContinental Journal of Archaeology* 31, no. 1 (2006): 165–202.

13. Edmunds, *The Potawatomi*, 227.

14. A complete history of the Black Hawk War can be found in Kerry A. Trask, *Black Hawk: Battle for the Heart of America* (New York: Henry Holt, 2007).

15. Donald Jackson, ed., *Black Hawk: An Autobiography* (Urbana: The University of Illinois Press, 1990), 49, 139.

16. Lurie, *Wisconsin Indians*, 20–21.

17. James A. Clifton, *The Prairie People: Continuity and Change in Potawatomi Culture, 1665–1965* (Lawrence: Regent Press of Kansas, 1977), 280–283.

18. Loew, *Indian Nations of Wisconsin*, 23–39, 59–98; Lurie, *Wisconsin Indians*, 5–10.

19. Loew, *Indian Nations of Wisconsin*, 50.

20. Ibid.

21. Ibid., 53.

22. United States Bureau of Indian Affairs, Census Roll of Wisconsin Potawatomi in Canada and the US, 1907. Records of the Bureau of Indian Affairs, Record Group 75, Wooster Roll, Special Series A, Box 2, National Archives and Records Administration, Washington, DC.

23. William Elsey Connelley, ed., "The Prairie Band of Pottawatomie Indians," *Collections of the Kansas State Historical Society 1915–1918*, vol. 14 (1918): 488–570.

24. Annual Report of the Commissioner of Indian Affairs (ARCOIA) (Washington, DC: US Government Printing Office, 1901), 244.

25. Clifton, *The Prairie People*, 382–383.

26. Annual Report of the Commissioner of Indian Affairs (ARCOIA) (Washington, DC: US Government Printing Office, 1872), 409–410.

27. Annual Report of the Commissioner of Indian Affairs (ARCOIA) (Washington, DC: US Government Printing Office, 1889), 216.

28. United States Indian Service Superintendent W. W. Burnett to Alphonse Gerend, July 29, 1918, Charles E. Brown Papers, Box 3, Potawatomi File, Wisconsin Historical Society Archives, Madison, WI.

NOTES TO CHAPTER 3

1. Thomas Vennum, *The Ojibwa Dance Drum: Its History and Construction*, Rev. ed. (Minneapolis: Minnesota Historical Society Press, 2009).

2. Ibid.

3. James A. Clifton, *The Prairie People: Continuity and Change in Potawatomi Culture, 1665–1965* (Lawrence: Regent Press of Kansas, 1977), 383; E. Stephens, Menominee Reservation, to the Commissioner of Indian Affairs, June 18 and 19, August 23, 1881, Record Group 75, National Archives, Washington, DC.

4. Benjamin G. Armstrong, *Early Life among the Indians* (Ashland, WI: A.W. Bowran, 1992), 156–160.

5. Vennum, *The Ojibwa Dance Drum*, 51–61.

6. Ibid., 202–203.

7. Ibid., 185

8. Ibid., 78–79, 88–92.

9. Ibid.

10. Alphonse Gerend, "Traditions and Customs of the Once Powerful Indian Tribes That Roamed over the State of Wisconsin," *The Sheboygan Press*, May 28, 1932.

11. Samuel A. Barrett, "The Dream Dance of the Chippewa and Menominee Indians of Northern Wisconsin," *Bulletin of the Public Museum of Milwaukee* 1 (1911): 252–402.

12. Vennum, *The Ojibwa Dance Drum*, 143–144.

13. John Gillin, "Acquired Drives in Cultural Contact," *American Anthropologist* 44 (1942): 552.

14. *Indian Dancing*, supplement to Circular No. 1665, February 14, 1923, Office of Indians Affairs, Department of Interior, Washington, DC.

15. George T. Amour, "A Personal Account: My Birthplace, McCord Indian Village." McCord site file, Office of the State Archaeologist, Wisconsin Historical Society, Madison, WI.

16. Vennum, *The Ojibwa Dance Drum*, 125–126.

17. Ibid.

18. Ibid.

19. Barrett, "The Dream Dance of the Chippewa and Menominee Indians."

20. Anthony F. C. Wallace, "Revitalization Movements," *American Antiquity* 58 (1956): 264–281.

21. Anthony F. C. Wallace, "Origins of the Longhouse Religion," *Handbook of North America Indians*, vol. 15, ed. Bruce G. Trigger (Washington, DC: Smithsonian Institution, 1978), 442–449.

22. Omer Stewart, *The Peyote Religion: A History* (Norman: University of Oklahoma Press, 1987).

23. John Sugden, *Tecumseh: A Life* (New York: Holt, 1997).

24. William Warren, *History of the Ojibwe Nation* (Minneapolis: Ross and Haines, 1972), 12.

25. Alice Beck Kehoe, *The Ghost Dance: Ethnohistory and Revitalization* (Long Grove, IL: Waveland Press, 2006).

26. Dee Brown, *Bury My Heart at Wounded Knee* (New York: Holt, Rinehart, and Winston, 1970), 439–445.

NOTES TO CHAPTER 4

1. "Indian Scare," *Burnett County Sentinel*, June 21, 1878; "The Wisconsin Scare: Report of the Adjutant-General—All the Rumors Caused by New Indian Dance," *New York Times*, June 25, 1878; Truman Michelson, "Final Notes on the Central Algonquian Dream Dance," *American Anthropologist* 28, no. 3 (1928): 373–376. The St. Croix Ojibwe had been overlooked by the 1854 Treaty of La Pointe that established Wisconsin Ojibwe reservations and remained landless until the 1930s. See Patty Loew, *Indian Nations of Wisconsin: Histories of Endurance and Renewal*, 2nd ed. (Madison: Wisconsin Historical Society Press, 2013), 82–84.

2. Eliza Morrison, *A Little History of My Forest Life*, ed. Victoria Brehm (Tustin, MI: Ladyslipper Press, 2002), 104–107.

3. Benjamin G. Armstrong, *Early Life among the Indians* (Ashland, WI: A.W. Bowran, 1992), 156–160.

4. Tom Jones, Michael Schmudlach, Matthew Daniel Mason, Amy Lonetree, and George A. Greendeer, *People of the Big Voice: Photographs of Ho-Chunk Families by Charles Van Schaick, 1879–1942* (Madison: Wisconsin Historical Society Press, 2011), 103.

5. Albert Thunder, "John Young," Charles E. Brown Papers, Box 3, Potawatomi File, Wisconsin Historical Society Archives, Madison, WI.

6. James A. Clifton, *The Prairie People: Continuity and Change in Potawatomi Culture, 1665–1965* (Lawrence: Regent Press of Kansas, 1977), 394.

7. Alphonse Gerend, "Traditions and Customs of the Once Powerful Indian Tribes That Roamed Over the State of Wisconsin," *Sheboygan Press*, May 28, 1932.

8. Ibid.

9. Ibid.

10. Town of Day Centennial Committee, *Town of Day, 101 Years, 1881–1982*, (Rosellville, WI: Centennial Committe, 1982), 156.

11. Map of the County of Marathon, Bussell and Holway, Civil Engineers, 1882, Wisconsin Historical Society Archives, Madison, WI.

12. Gerend, "Traditions and Customs."

13. Ibid.

14. Annual Report of the Commissioner of Indian Affairs (ARCOIA), (Washington, DC: US Government Printing Office, 1884): 102.

15. Clifton, *The Prairie People*, 385.

16. Annual Report of the Commissioner of Indian Affairs (ARCOIA) (Washington, DC: US Government Printing Office, 1889): 216.

17. Burnett County Historical Society, "'Stray Bands' and Dream Dancers: Indian Farms and Potawatomi Settlement in Central Wisconsin during the 19th and 20th Century." Grant Report submitted to the Historic Preservation Division, Wisconsin Historical Society, Madison, WI, 1986; Mark Bruhy, "Big

Indian Farm Site (Site No. 09-02-03-001)" and "Little Indian Farm Site, (09-02-03-002)," Cultural Resource Site Inspection, 1985 report on file, USDA Forest Service, Rhinelander, WI.

18. "Greenfield Leaves," *Taylor County Star and News* (Medford), August 8, 1896; "Localisms," *Taylor County Star and News* (Medford), July 21, 1896.

19. "Localisms," *Taylor County Star and News* (Medford), August 7, 1897.

20. Untitled, *Taylor County Star and News* (Medford), March 17, 1905.

21. Roy Speils, "Oral History of Indian Farms," interview by US Forest Service, September 13, 1977, Rhinelander, Wisconsin; Annual Report of the Commissioner of Indian Affairs (ARCOIA) (Washington, DC: US Government Printing Office, 1901): 244.

22. Michael R. Albert, Kristen G. Ostheimer, and Joel G. Breman, "The Last Smallpox Epidemic in Boston and the Vaccination Controversy, 1901–1903," *New England Journal of Medicine* 344 (2001), 375–379.

23. "Small Pox," *Taylor County Star and News*, March 23, 1901; Tom Jones, "A Ho-Chunk Photographer Looks at Charles Van Schaick," in Jones, *People of the Big Voice*, 26.

24. ARCOIA, 1901: 244.

25. Diane Young Holliday, National Register Nomination for McCord Indian Village, November 2000, Division of Historic Preservation, Wisconsin Historical Society, Madison, WI.

26. Publius Lawson, "The Potawatomi," *The Wisconsin Archeologist* 19 (1920): 103–104.

27. George T. Armour, "A Personal Account: My Birthplace, McCord Indian Village." McCord site file, Office of the State Archaeologist, Wisconsin Historical Society, Madison, WI.

28. Matthew M. Thomas, "Where the Forest Meets the Farm: A Comparison of the Spatial and Historic Change in the Euro-American and American Indian Maple Sugar Landscape," PhD diss., University of Wisconsin–Madison, 2004; Matthew M. Thomas, "Historic American Indian Maple Sugar and Syrup Production: Boiling Arches in Michigan and Wisconsin," *Midcontinental Journal of Archaeology* 30 (2005): 299–326.

NOTES TO CHAPTER 5

1. James A. Clifton, *The Prairie People: Continuity and Change in Potawatomi Culture, 1665–1965* (Lawrence: Regent Press of Kansas, 1977), 403.

2. Scott to Commissioner of Indian Affairs, October 7, 15, and 31, 1892, Federal Records Center, Kansas City, Missouri, cited in Clifton, *The Prairie People*, 395.

3. Annual Report of the Commissioner of Indian Affairs (ARCOIA) (Washington, DC: US Government Printing Office, 1920), Appendix K, 93.

4. Publius Lawson, "The Potawatomi," *The Wisconsin Archeologist* 19 (1920): 41–116; "The Indians Dance," *Pittsville Record*, October 14, 1909.

5. Video of interviews with elders at Skunk Hill filmed by Randy Snowball, Wisconsin Rapids, WI, August 20, 2005.

6. Alphonse Gerend, "Traditions and Customs of the Once Powerful Indian Tribes That Roamed over the State of Wisconsin," *Sheboygan Press*, May 28, 1932.

7. David Engel, "After All These Years, 'Skunk Hill' Stands Tall," *Daily Tribune* (Wisconsin Rapids), May 12, 1984.

8. George O. Jones, *History of Wood County, Wisconsin* (Minneapolis: H.C. Cooper Jr. and Company, 1923), 236.

9. Engel, "After All These Years, 'Skunk Hill' Stands Tall."

10. Jones, *History of Wood County*, 236.

11. "Berry Picking Time Is Busy Time for the Indian Race," *Daily Tribune* (Wisconsin Rapids), July 23, 1924.

12. David Engel, "Skunk Hill's Sacred Rituals," *Daily Tribune* (Wisconsin Rapids), May 19, 1884.

13. "Big Land Claim," *Daily Tribune* (Grand Rapids, WI), September 12, 1906.

14. Wood County Register of Deeds, Wood County Courthouse, Wisconsin Rapids, WI; *Standard Atlas of Wood County* (Chicago: George Ogle and Company, 1909); *Standard Atlas of Wood County* (Chicago: Brock and Company, 1920, 1928).

15. William Elsey Connelley, ed., "The Prairie Band of Pottawatomie Indians," *Collections of the Kansas State Historical Society, 1915–1918* 14 (1918): 555–570.

16. Gerend, "Traditions and Customs."

17. Alphonse Gerend, Photographic Albums, 2 vols., Wisconsin Historical Society Archives, Madison, WI.

18. Norm Severt, interview by Catherine Woodward, 2000, Skunk Hill/Powers Bluff file, Office of the State Archaeologist, Division of Historic Preservation, Wisconsin Historical Society, Madison, WI.

19. Lyle Hamel, personal communication with author, 2000.

20. "Indian Graveyard on Powers Bluff," *Daily Tribune* (Wisconsin Rapids), July 3, 1936.

21. Lyle Hamel, personal communication with author, 2003; interview with Graham family by Robert Birmingham, 2000; Engel, "Skunk Hill's Sacred Rituals."

22. George Christiansen, "Expanded Phase I Archaeological Survey of a Portion of Powers Bluff, Wood County, Wisconsin," Archaeological Research, Inc., 2002, Powers Bluff/Skunk Hill file, Office of the State Archaeologist, Wisconsin Historical Society, Madison, WI.

23. James A. Clifton, "Potawatomi," *Handbook of North America Indians*, vol. 15, ed., Bruce G. Trigger (Washington, DC: Smithsonian Institution, 1978).

24. Gerend, "Traditions and Customs."

25. Annual Report of the Grand Rapids Indian Agency, 1919. Records of the Bureau of Indian Affairs, Grand Rapids Indian Agency, Record Group 75, National Archives and Record Service Services, Washington, DC.

26. University of Oregon, Mapping History, http:// mappinghistory.uoregon.edu/english/US/US39-01.html.

27. Death Certificate for Waub-Mee-Mee (White Pigeon), 1931, Wood County Courthouse, Wisconsin Rapids, Wisconsin.

28. Gerend, "Traditions and Customs."

29. Ibid.

30. Engel, "Skunk Hill's Sacred Rituals."

31. Gerend, "Traditions and Customs."

32. Alanson Skinner, "The Mascoutens or Prairie Potawatomi," *Bulletin of the Public Museum of Milwaukee* 6, no. 1 (1924): 1–261.

33. Gerend, "Traditions and Customs."

34. Ibid.

35. Ibid.

36. Ibid.

37. Ibid.

38. Ibid.

39. "The Indian Dance," *The State Center* (Vesper, WI), October 10, 1912.

40. Ibid.

41. Gerend, "Traditions and Customs."

42. Ibid.

43. Daniel Shepard to Charles E. Brown, June 28, 1928, Charles E. Brown Papers, Box 48, Wisconsin Historical Society Archives, Madison, WI.

44. Plat book of Wood County, 1948, Marathon Map Service, Milwaukee, WI.

45. Video of interviews with elders at Skunk Hill filmed by Randy Snowball, 2005.

46. Ibid.

47. For example, the Wood County Register of Deeds (Wood County Courthouse, Wisconsin Rapids, WI) indicates that ten-acre parcels purchased from "C E King and Wife" by Shau wa quouk (sic) (Warranty Deed, 6/16/1914, vol. 86, p. 354), Mixtqua and Keo Komequah (sic) (Warranty Deed, 6/16/1914, vol. 86, p. 426), and Squagishgoquah and Shohm (sic) (Warranty Deed, 6/16/1914, vol. 86, p. 427) passed to H. F. Roerhing sometime prior to 1933, but there are no deed recording the transfers. The Town of Arpin acquired these lands, with adjacent parcels, from Elizabeth Roehring and the H. F. Roehring estate with tax and quit claim deeds (vol. 157, p. 44; vol. 158, p. 70). Wood County acquired the lands from the Town of Arpin, along with adjacent parcels, in 1936 for one dollar to be used as a county park (Quit Claim Deed, 10/27/1936, vol. 161, p. 508).

48. Wood County Register of Deeds Records, Wisconsin Rapids, WI, Warranty Deed, John Louie (10 acres) to H. F. Roehring, 2/21/1927, vol. 140, p. 294.

49. Rick St. Germain, "Afterword," in Thomas Vennum, *The Ojibwe Dance Drum: Its History and Construction*, Rev. ed. (St. Paul: Minnesota Historical Society Press, 2009), 319–329.

NOTES TO CHAPTER 6

1. Tax deed between Town of Arpin and H. F. Roehring Estate, December 13, 1933, vol. 158, p. 70, Wood County Register of Deeds Records, Wisconsin Rapids, WI; Quit Claim Deed between Elizabeth Roehring and Town of Arpin, December 13, 1933, vol. 157, p. 44, Wood County Register of Deeds Records, Wisconsin Rapids, WI; "Powers Bluff, Early Indian Camp Site, Now County Park," *Daily Tribune* (Wisconsin Rapids), July 3, 1936. See also David Engel, "After All These Years 'Skunk Hill' Still Stands Tall," *Daily Tribune* (Wisconsin Rapids), May 12, 1984; David Engel, "Skunk Hill's Sacred Rituals," *Daily Tribune* (Wisconsin Rapids), May 19, 1984.

2. For example, Susan Lampert Smith, "Tree Clearing on Hill Cuts Deep," *Wisconsin State Journal*, Madison, WI, April 5, 2001.

3. Robert A. Birmingham, "Preliminary Report on Powers Bluff, 2000," Archaeological Survey of Zone I, Powers Bluff, 2001; Robert A. Birmingham, National Register Nomination for *Tahqua-kik* or Skunk Hill, 2002; Robert Boszhardt, "Letter Report on Archaeological Survey of North Slope and West of Lower Cemetery, Notes and Maps." Mississippi Valley Archaeological Center, La Crosse, WI, 2001; George Christiansen, "Results of Expanded Phase I Archaeological Investigation of a Portion of Powers Bluff, Wood County, Wisconsin," Archaeological Research, Inc., Madison, WI, 2002; Matthew M. Thomas, "Letter Report on Inspection of Maple Trees Possibly Tapped in the Past for Maple Sap, 2001;" Don Johnson, "Powers Bluff Geophysical Investigation," Hemisphere Field Services, Minneapolis, MN, 2001; David Maki, "Geophysical Investigation of Powers Bluff Cemetery and Historic Village, Archaeo-Physics Reports of Investigation #27," Minneapolis, MN, 2001. All reports on file, Power's Bluff/Skunk Hill file, Office of the State Archaeologist, Division of Historic Preservation, Wisconsin Historical Society, Madison, WI.

4. Anita Clark, "Skunk Hill Honor Hailed, Indians Applaud as Bluff Designated a State Historic Site," *Wisconsin State Journal* (Madison), April 13, 2002.

5. Adam Campbell, "Skunk Hill Sacred to American Indian Religion," *Native American News*, http://people.uwec.edu/mdorsher/NativeNews/campbell2.htm.

6. Powers Bluff County Park Long Range Master Plan, Schrieber and Associates, 2005, Wood County Parks and Recreation, Wisconsin Rapids, WI.

Bibliography

Articles, Books, Reports

Albert, Michael R., Kristen G. Ostheimer, and Joel G. Breman, "The Last Smallpox Epidemic in Boston and the Vaccination Controversy, 1901–1903." *New England Journal of Medicine* 344 (2001): 375–379.

Annual Report of the Commissioner of Indian Affairs. Washington, DC: US Government Printing Office, 1872, 1884, 1889, 1901, 1920.

Armstrong, Benjamin G. *Early Life among the Indians.* Ashland, WI: A.W. Bowran, 1992.

Arpin 1873–1973: Centennial. Amherst, WI: Helbach Printing, 1973.

Barrett, Samuel A. "The Dream Dance of the Chippewa and Menominee Indians of Northern Wisconsin." *Bulletin of the Public Museum of Milwaukee* I (1911): 252–371.

Birmingham, Robert A. "Preliminary Report on Powers Bluff, 2000." Archaeological Survey of Zone I, Powers Bluff, 2001. Report on file, Powers Bluff/Skunk Hill file, Office of the State Archaeologist, Division of Historic Preservation, Wisconsin Historical Society, Madison, WI.

———. *Tah-qua-kik or Skunk Hill.* National Register Nomination on file, 2002, Division of Historic Preservation, Wisconsin Historical Society.

Bonvillian, Nancy. *Native Nations of North America.* New York: Pearson, 2001.

Boszhardt, Robert. "Letter Report on Archaeological Survey of Powers Bluff North Slope and West of Lower Cemetery, Notes and Maps." Mississippi Valley Archaeological Center, La Crosse, WI, 2001. Power's Bluff/Skunk Hill file, Office of the State Archaeologist, Division of Historic Preservation, Wisconsin Historical Society, Madison, WI.

Brookings Institution. *The Problem of Indian Administration: Report of a Survey made at the request of Honorable Hubert Work, Secretary of the Interior, and submitted to him, February 21, 1928, Baltimore, Md.* Baltimore: The Johns Hopkins Press, 1928.

Brown, Dee. *Bury My Heart at Wounded Knee.* New York: Holt, Rinehart, and Winston, 1970.

Bruhy, Mark. "Big Indian Farm Site (Site No. 09-02-03-001)." Cultural Resource Site Inspection, 1985. Report on File, USDA Forest Service, Rhinelander, WI.

———. "Little Indian Farm Site (09-02-03-002)." Cultural Resource Site Inspection, 1985. Report on File, USDA Forest Service, Rhinelander, WI.

Burnett County Historical Society. "'Stray Bands' and Dream Dancers: Indian Farms and Potawatomi Settlement in Central Wisconsin During the 19th and 20th Century." Grant report submitted to the Historic Preservation Division, Wisconsin Historical Society, Madison, WI, 1986.

Campbell, Adam. "Skunk Hill Sacred to American Indian Religion," *Native American News,* http://people.uwec.edu/mdorsher/NativeNews/campbell2.htm.

Christiansen, George. "Results of Expanded Phase I Archaeological Survey Investigation of a Portion of Powers Bluff, Wood County, Wisconsin." Archaeological Research Inc. 2002. Powers Bluff/Skunk Hill file, Office of the State Archaeologist, Wisconsin Historical Society, Madison, WI.

Clifton, James A. "Potawatomi." *Handbook of North America Indians: Northeast,* vol. 15, ed. Bruce G. Trigger. Washington, DC: Smithsonian Institution, 1978. 725–42.

———. "Sociocultural Dynamics of the Prairie Potawatomi Drum Dance." *Plains Anthropologist* 14 no. 44 (1969): 85–93.

———. "Wisconsin Death March: Explaining the Extremes in Old Northwest Indian Removal." *Transactions of the Wisconsin Academy of Sciences, Arts and Letters* 75 (1987): 1–40.

———. *The Prairie People: Continuity and Change in Potawatomi Indian Culture, 1665–1965.* Lawrence, Kansas: Regents Press of Kansas, 1977.

Collins, Douglas. *The Story of Kodak.* New York: Henry N. Abrams, 1990.

Connelley, William Elsey, ed. "The Prairie Band of Pottawatomie Indians." *Collections of the Kansas State Historical Society, 1915–1918,* vol. 14, (1918): 488–570.

Edmonds, David. *The Potawatomi: Keepers of the Fire.* Norman: University of Oklahoma Press, 1987.

Gillin, John. "Acquired Drives in Culture Contact." *American Anthropologist* 44 (1942): 545–554.

Hickerson, Harold. "The Southwestern Chippewa: An Ethnohistorical Study." *American Anthropological Association* 64, no. 3, part 2 (1962): 1–110.

Hill, G., J. Biersack, V. Thums, P. Ochodnicky, and J. Spieles. *Westboro 1875–1975: Pages of History.* Westboro, WI: Westboro Centennial Committee, 1975.

Hirsh, Mark. "Thomas Jefferson: Founding Father of Indian Removal." *National Museum of the American Indian* 11, no. 2 (2009): 54–58.

Hoelscher, Steven D. *Picturing Indians.* Madison: University of Wisconsin Press, 2008.

Holliday, Diane Young. National Register Nomination for McCord Indian Village, Division of Historic Preservation, November 2000, Wisconsin Historical Society, Madison, WI.

Jackson, Donald, ed. *Black Hawk: An Autobiography.* 1964. Urbana: University of Illinois Press, 1990.

Jahoda, Gloria. *Trail of Tears: The Story of the American Indian Removal, 1813–1855.* New York: Henry Holt, 1995.

Johnson, Don. "Powers Bluff Geophysical Investigation." Hemisphere Field Services, Minneapolis, MN, 2001. Powers Bluff/Skunk Hill file, Office of the State Archaeologist, Division of Historic Preservation, Wisconsin Historical Society, Madison, WI.

Jones, George O. *History of Wood County, Wisconsin.* Minneapolis, MN: H.C. Cooper, Jr. & Company, 1923.

Jones, Tom, Michael Schmudlach, Matthew Daniel Mason, Amy Lonetree, and George A. Greendeer. *People of the Big Voice: Photographs of Ho-Chunk Families by Charles Van Schaick, 1879–1942.* Madison: Wisconsin Historical Society Press, 2011.

Kehoe, Alice Beck. *The Ghost Dance: Ethnohistory & Revitalization,* 2nd ed. Long Grove, IL: Waveland Press, 2006.

Lawson, Publius. "The Potawatomi." *The Wisconsin Archeologist* 19 (1920): 41–116.

Loew, Patty. *Indian Nations of Wisconsin: Histories of Endurance and Renewal,* 2nd edition, Madison, WI: Wisconsin Historical Society Press, 2013.

Lurie, Nancy Oestreich. *Wisconsin Indians*, rev. ed. Madison, WI: Wisconsin Historical Society Press, 2002.

Maki, David. Geophysical Investigation of Powers Bluff Cemetery and Historic Village, Archaeo-Physics Reports of Investigation no. 27, 2001. Minneapolis, Minnesota. Power's Bluff/Skunk Hill file, Office of the State Archaeologist, Division of Historic Preservation, Wisconsin Historical Society, Madison, WI.

McKenny, Thomas and James Hall. *History of the Indian Tribes of North America*, 3 Vol. Philadelphia: E.T. Biddle, 1848–1850.

Michelson, Truman. "Final Notes on the Central Algonquian Dream Dance." *American Anthropologist* 28, no. 3 (1926): 573–76.

Mitchell, Gary. "Tribal History." Prairie Band Potawatomi website, www.pbpindiantribe.com/tribal-history.aspx.

Morrison, Eliza. *A Little History of My Forest Life*. Victoria Brehm, ed. Tustin, MI: Ladyslipper Press, 2002.

Ritzenthaler, Robert E. "The Potawatomi Indians of Wisconsin." *Bulletin of the Public Museum of Milwaukee* 19, no. 3 (1953): 99–174.

Sasso, Robert F. and Dan Joyce. "Ethnohistory and Archaeology: The Removal Era Potawatomi Lifeway in Southeastern Wisconsin." *Midcontinental Journal of Archaeology* 31, no. 1 (2006): 165–202.

Schrieber and Associates. "Powers Bluff County Park Long Range Master Plan." Wood County Parks and Recreation, Wisconsin Rapids, WI, 2005.

Severt, Norm. Interview by Catherine Woodward. 2000. Powers Bluff/Powers Bluff file, Office of the State Archaeologist, Division of Historic Preservation, Wisconsin Historical Society, Madison, WI.

Skinner, Alanson. "The Mascoutens or Prairie Potawatomi." *Bulletin of the Public Museum of Milwaukee* 6, nos. 1–3 (1926): 9–411.

Speils, Roy. "Oral History of Indian Farms." Interview by US Forest Service, September 13, 1977. Rhinelander, WI.

Stewart, Omer. *The Peyote Religion: A History*. Norman: University of Oklahoma Press, 1987.

Sugden, John. *Tecumseh: A Life*. New York: Holt, 1997.

Town of Day Centennial Committee. *Town of Day, 101 Years, 1881–1982.* Centennial Committee: Rozellville, WI, 1982.

Thomas, Matthew M. "Letter report on inspection of maple trees possibility tapped in the past for maple sap, 2001." Report on file, Archaeological Site File, Power's Bluff/Skunk Hill (47-WO-0002), Office of the State Archaeologist, Division of Historical Preservation, Wisconsin Historical Society, Madison, WI.

———. "Historic American Indian Maple Sugar and Syrup Production: Boiling Arches in Michigan and Wisconsin." *Midcontinental Journal of Archaeology* 30 (2005): 299–326.

———. "Where the Forest Meets the Farm: A Comparison of the Spatial and Historic Change in the Euro-American and American Indian Maple Sugar Landscape." Ph.D. diss., University of Wisconsin–Madison, 2004.

Trask, Kerry A. *Black Hawk: The Battle for the Heart of America.* New York: Henry Holt, 2007.

Trigger, Bruce G., ed. *Handbook of North America Indians*, vol. 15. Washington, DC: Smithsonian Institution, 1978.

United States Office of Indian Affairs. Annual Report of the Commissioner of Indian Affairs. Office of Indian Affairs, Department of the Interior, Washington, DC: US Printing Office, 1872, 1884, 1889, 1901.

United States Office of Indian Affairs. *Indian Dancing.* Supplement to Circular No 1665. Office of Indians Affairs. Department of the Interior, Washington, DC: US Printing Office, 1923.

Vennum, Thomas. *The Ojibwa Dance Drum: Its History and Construction*, rev. ed. Saint Paul: Minnesota Historical Society Press, 2009.

Wallace, Anthony F. C. "Origins of the Longhouse Religion." *Handbook of North American Indians*, vol. 15, ed. Bruce

———. "Revitalization Movements." *American Anthropologist* 58 (1956): 264–81.

Warren, William. *History of the Ojibwe Nation.* Minneapolis, MN: Ross and Haines, 1972.

Welniak, Marie Karen. *100 Year History of Town of Richfield, Wood County, Wisconsin.* Marshfield, WI: Speedy Print, 1981.

Newspaper Articles

"Berry Picking Time is Busy Time for the Indian Race." *Daily Tribune* (Wisconsin Rapids), July 23, 1924.

"Big Land Claim." *Daily Tribune* (Wisconsin Rapids), September 12, 1906.

Clark, Anita. "Skunk Hill Honor Hailed, Indians Applaud as Bluff Designated a State Historic Site." *Wisconsin State Journal* (Madison), April 13, 2002.

Engel, David. "After All These Years 'Skunk Hill' Still Stands Tall," *Daily Tribune* (Wisconsin Rapids), May 12, 1984.

———. "Skunk Hill's Sacred Rituals." *Daily Tribune* (Wisconsin Rapids), May 19, 1984.

Gerend, Alphonse. "Traditions and Customs of the Once Powerful Indian Tribes that Roamed Over the State of Wisconsin." *Sheboygan Press*, May 28, 1932.

"Great Indian Scare." *Grand Rapids Tribune* (Grand Rapids, WI), June 28, 1878.

"Greenfield Leaves." *Taylor County Star and News* (Medford), August 8, 1896.

"Indian Graveyard on Powers Bluff." *Daily Tribune* (Wisconsin Rapids), July 3, 1936.

"Indian Scare." *Burnett County Sentinel* (Grantsburg), June 21, 1878.

"Indian Tradition." *Marshfield News* (Marshfield), Feb. 13, 1908

"Localisms." *Taylor County Star and News* (Medford), July 21, 1897.

"Localisms." *Taylor County Star and News* (Medford), August 7, 1897.

"On the Old Trails." *Marshfield News* (Marshfield), December 6, 1906.

"Power's Bluff, Early Indian Camp Site, Now County Park." *Daily Tribune* (Wisconsin Rapids), July 3, 1936.

"Small Pox." *Taylor County Star and News* (Medford), March 23, 1901.

Smith, Susan Lampert. "Tree Clearing on Hill Cuts Deep." *Wisconsin State Journal* (Madison), April 5, 2001.

"The Indian Dance." *The State Center* (Vesper), October 10, 1912.

"The Indians Dance," *Pittsville Record*, October 14, 1909.

"The Wisconsin Scare: Report of the Adjutant-General All the Rumors Caused by New Indian Dance." *New York Times*, June 25, 1878.

Archival Sources

Amour, George T. "A Personal Account: My Birthplace, McCord Indian Village." One page manuscript, McCord Site File, Office of the State Archaeologist, Wisconsin Historical Society, Madison, WI.

Annual Report of the Grand Rapids Indian Agency, 1919. Records of the Bureau of Indian Affairs, Grand Rapids Indian Agency, Record Group 75, National Archives and Record Service Services, Washington, DC.

Charles E. Brown Papers, 1889–1945. Wisconsin Historical Society Archives, Madison, WI.

Gerend, Alphonse, Photographic Albums, 2 vols. Wisconsin Historical Society Archives, Madison, WI.

Map of the County of Marathon. Bussel and Holway, Civil Engineers, 1882. Wisconsin Historical Society Archives, Madison, WI.

Ownership Plat Book of Wood County. Milwaukee: Marathon Map Service, 1948.

Standard Atlas of Wood County. Chicago: George Ogle and Company, 1909.

Standard Atlas of Wood County. Chicago: Brock and Company, 1920, 1928.

Thirteenth Census of the United States, Arpin Township, Wood County, Wisconsin, Special Inquiries Relating to Indians, 1910. National Archives and Records Administration, Washington, DC.

United States Bureau of Indian Affairs. Census Roll of Wisconsin Potawatomi in Canada and the US, 1907. Records of the Bureau of Indian Affairs, Record Group 75, Wooster Roll, Special Series A, Box 2, National Archives and Records Administration, Washington, DC.

Wood County Register of Deeds. Wood County Courthouse, Wisconsin Rapids, WI.

Index

About the Author

Robert A. Birmingham served as Wisconsin State Archaeologist at the Wisconsin Historical Society and teaches at the University of Wisconsin–Waukesha. Among other books, he is the author of *Life, Death, and Archaeology at Fort Blue Mounds* and coauthor of *Indian Mounds of Wisconsin* and *Aztalan: Mysteries of an Ancient Indian Town*, which received a merit award for history from the Midwest Independent Publishers Association. He has been researching Drum Dance communities for over 30 years and has worked with descendants of Skunk Hill, the Prairie Potowatomi Nation, and many others to document its history.